THE GAMBLING TIMES
GUIDE TO
CASINO GAMES

LEN MILLER

A GAMBLING TIMES BOOK
DISTRIBUTED BY CAROL PUBLISHING

Library of Congress Cataloging in Publication Data

MILLER, LEN
THE GAMBLING TIMES GUIDE TO CASINO GAMES

ISBN: 0-89746-071-5

Manufactured in the United States of America

Carol Publishing Group Edition 1997

Distributed by Carol Publishing Group
120 Enterprise Avenue
Secaucus, N.J. 07094

In Canada: Canadian Manda Group,
One Atlantic Avenue, Suite 105,
Toronto, Ontario M6K 3E7

Carol Publishing Group books may be purchased in bulk at special discounts for sales promotions, fund-raising, or educational purposes. Special editions can be created to specifications. For details, contact Special Sales Department, Carol Publishing Group, 120 Enterprise Avenue, Secaucus, N.J. 07094

All material presented in this book is offered as information to the reader. No inducement to gamble is intended or implied.

ACKNOWLEDGEMENTS

The author wishes to thank the following *Gambling Times* staff members for their help and assistance in producing this book: *Arnold L. Abrams*—Executive Production Manager, Book Division; *Jerrold Kazdoy*—Editorial Production Manager, Book Division; *Joanne Gutreimen*—Editorial Researcher; and *David B. James* and *Andrea Pollock*—Composition.

TABLE OF CONTENTS

PREFACE

Before we discuss the individual casino games we play for fun and profit, I would like to introduce you to casino gaming in general. In my years as editor of *Gambling Times* magazine, I have had the opportunity to visit all of the casinos in Atlantic City, Las Vegas, Reno, and Lake Tahoe, in addition to other gaming areas. Without slighting the glamour, beauty, and historical background of the European casinos that I have also visited, I must say that the American casinos provide the best possible atmosphere for the player.

It is simple and easy to play at any of the casino tables here: the milieu is more informal, and one can enter and leave a game at will. If you have winning chips to cash in, the attendants at the cashiers cage count your chips and pay you in cash, with a smile. If you win a large amount of money, you will be offered the courtesy of a safety deposit box, or the casino cashier will give you a receipt for as much money as you wish to leave for safekeeping.

By and large, the casinos extend a good deal of courtesy and respect to the players. If you are a big player you may receive complimentary dinners, show reservations, and even hotel accommodations. Almost all of the casinos, small and large alike, serve complimentary drinks to the players. (A word of advice here: Although you are obviously at a casino-resort hotel for a good time, it would be wise to confine your drinking to after you've finished playing and have left the tables.)

Without question, these resorts provide the very best in outdoor and indoor amenities. Swimming pools, tennis courts, golf courses, and even bowling are available to vacationers. Most holiday-seekers combine these fun activities into their schedule. The superior quality and diversity of entertainment offered in each hotel is scarcely available anywhere else in the world. Food is also lavishly offered in a number of dining areas, including coffee shops, buffets, and gourmet restaurants. There definitely is something for everyone's taste in these beautiful casino-resort complexes.

Of course, we all agree that it's the casinos' gambling profits that pay for all of this. But, some people *do* win and that is why you are reading this book. You can be one of those who walk away from the casino with profits to take home. When you do, you'll be among the 10% or so who do win. That's just fine with the casinos—they like those percentages: 90% losers, 10% winners.

In all fairness, though, the casinos are not responsible for anyone losing. All the casinos do is provide a beautiful game floor with the various games attended by dealers. They admittedly have a built-in advantage, a percentage in their favor. Those percentages may not be known to most of the players but, luckily for you, these figures will become part of your overall knowledge. Possessing this information will give you a decided edge over those 90% of the people who lose enough to pay for all the overhead in the casinos and provide a tidy profit for management.

Let me stress that learning the right way to play casino games is much the same as learning how to play bridge, chess, backgammon or even how to properly hold a tennis racket. There is no sure way of winning all of the time, and there definitely is an element of luck and timing involved in most of the games, but there is also a *right* way to play each game.

Your attitude is all-important in becoming a winning player. In fact, your attitude sets the stage for how well you accept and follow the principles set forth in this book. Obviously, some people can read the same text and get more out of what they read and learn than others reading the same material.

Casino games are fun and exciting to play. Competition is the key word, especially when you've got your money on the line against the adversary: the casino. You are now going to learn to compete against the table at whatever game you're playing. The competition ends when you walk away from the game; let's see if we can make you a winner most of those times.

FOREWORD

In any sporting game such as tennis, golf, bowling, etc., a good part of winning lies in strength, endurance, and other forms of physical prowess. Yet, even in those games, a good part of winning also has to do with awareness, psychological advantage, being sharp, and looking for an edge.

In more passive games such as bridge, chess, backgammon, gin rummy and poker, physical attributes are not that important. In fact, the most needed physical qualifications are to be well rested and mentally alert.

In those card games just mentioned, skill is the main requirement for winning. Becoming a better player in any game, and then expanding that expertise each time you play or practice, is the best winning formula I know of.

The games discussed in this "how-to" manual are available in the gaming casinos in Nevada, Atlantic City, and throughout the world.

Over the past few years, readers of *Gambling Times* magazine have learned that there are better ways to play *any* game. By playing *better*, the gamer has a greater chance of winning more, and losing less. *That in effect is the crux of the entire matter.* Becoming a more knowledgeable player of any game gives one a feeling of confidence that contributes to winning.

Learning the rules and procedures of playing each game, and becoming totally conversant with those regulations, is the first important step. I can hardly think of anyone disagreeing with that statement. And yet, a large percentage of casino players are not totally familiar with the rules and procedures of the games they play. Once you have mastered these prerequisites, you'll find that playing the games becomes pleasant, entertaining and fun!

So there you have it. When you finish reading this book, you'll be able to enjoy your gaming sojourns better than ever. Best of all, it's yours to read over again and to keep as a handy source of reference.

Yours for winning,

Len Miller

Chapter 1
<u>Craps</u>: From Basic to Expert

Craps is the fast-moving, action-filled game that is so often identified with high rollers. As you may know, "high roller" is the name given to big money players. Many of these $100-chip bettors walk into a craps game with a credit line ranging from $5000 to $100,000.

The great thing about playing craps is that the $2 or $5 bettor stands right alongside the high roller and shares the fun and excitement of the game in the same manner. In many cases, the player starting out with $50 in chips and making small bets may walk away from the table with anywhere from $500 to $1500 in profits, while the high roller may still be writing markers trying to recoup his losses.

That scenario can apply to you and your own $50 bankroll if you pay close attention to this chapter and practice what you learn.

Although one may walk up to a craps table and become befuddled by all of the action going on, craps is really quite simple to learn. The name, incidentally, is always called craps: You shoot craps, you're a craps shooter and, ironically, if you roll craps you lose!

The Roll of the Dice

Craps is a dice game played with dice. *It is a game of chance!* There is no skill in shooting craps. Each time the dice are rolled, the probabilities of any set of numbers coming out are always exactly the same.

That is your first lesson. The paragraph above cannot be disputed. So don't fight it—believe it. If a shooter makes a 7 on his first roll, and another 7 on the next roll, there is no reason to say he can't win on the third roll. The chance of rolling a 7 on any given roll is exactly six chances in 36. Significantly, the 7 comes up, or rather has a chance of coming up, on any roll more than any other number. Diagram 1-1 shows the 36 rolls and the odds probability of each pairing:

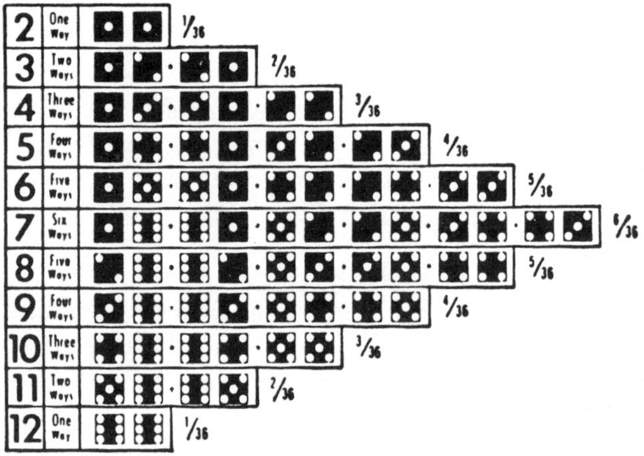

Diagram 1-1

Actually, there are only 11 different numbers (pairings) that can be rolled. As you can see in Diagram 1-1, while there is just one way to roll a 2, and only one way to roll a 12, there are two ways to make a 3 or 11, three ways for a 4 and 10, four ways to roll a 5 or 9, five ways for a 6 and 8, and six ways to make a 7.

* * *

This clearly shows the math of craps. While each roll of the dice can produce any of those 11 numbers, and although the probabilities are clearly stated, it is also true that the number 12 could come up on two consecutive rolls. If you bet a $5 chip on 12 and it came up on that roll you would receive $150 as your payoff. If you let that amount ride—that is, bet the $150 on 12 for the next roll—and if it repeated as I stated above, you would receive the whopping sum of $4500.

By the same token, betting on the 12 is something I strongly suggest not doing. It and other bets like it are too advantageous for the house, as you will learn from what you read here.

An Introduction to Craps

The game of craps is easy to learn and play. The rules are simple to follow. It's a fun game that can add considerable enjoyment to your gambling holiday. And even though most young ladies may not have played craps during their youth, casino bank craps is as much a game for women as it is for men.

The difference between a private game of craps and casino bank craps is this: In the former, there is no bank. A shooter puts some money down and another player or players *fade* him. The player is betting he will win, the *faders* are betting he will lose. The shooter picks up the dice and rolls them. When rolling the dice, the same rules apply the world over. That is, the mechanics of the game are the same in a private game as they are in a casino bank game. The only material difference is that players are betting against each other.

In a casino bank game, the players place their bets and the casino bank *fades* them. In addition to covering every player's bet *(cover* has now replaced the term *fade),* the casino bank craps game offers many other types of proposition bets. These bets, along with the basic *pass* and *don't pass* bets, are explained in Diagram 1-2.

As you will note, there are four people actively running the game. The *boxman,* sitting behind the table in the middle, is the boss. It is his duty to watch each roll of the dice and keep his eyes constantly on the game. The two dealers, one to each side of him, pay off the players when they win and rake in their chips when they lose. Each dealer handles all the players on his side. The table is divided by the center box of *proposition* bets and also by the *stickman,* who stands on the players' side of the table.

The players stand around the table, usually three or four at each end and four to six on either side of the stickman.

The stickman controls the action of the dice as well as the pace of the game. After seeing all bets are down, the stickman pushes a

COME

Come bets simply mean that a player is betting with the dice exactly as on the pass line, except that come bets are made any time after the shooter has established a point. Players win on natural 7 or 11 and lose on craps 2, 3 and 12. Any number that comes up is the come point. As on a pass-line bet, players win if that number appears before 7 is rolled.

DON'T COME

The play is again reversed. A player is betting after a point has been established on the line. A player is betting against the dice exactly as on the don't-pass line. If natural 7 or 11 appear a player loses. He wins on craps 2 or 3. When a 12 is rolled, it's a standoff. If a 4, 5, 6, 8, 9 or 10 comes up after the point has been established, the player loses if the shooter makes that point on any subsequent rolls. The player wins if a 7 is rolled before the number shows again.

ANY 7—This is a one—roll bet. Player bets that the next roll is a 7. Pays 5 for 1.

BUY BETS

Player may buy a place bet (do or don't) by paying 5% vigorish. FULL odds then prevail.

PLACE BETS

Players may make place bets on 4, 5, 6, 8, 9 or 10. To win the place bet the number must show before a 7 is thrown. The payoff is 9 to 5 on 4 and 10, 7 to 5 on 5 and 9, 7 to 6 on 6 and 8. When placing the DON'T, you lay the reverse odds.

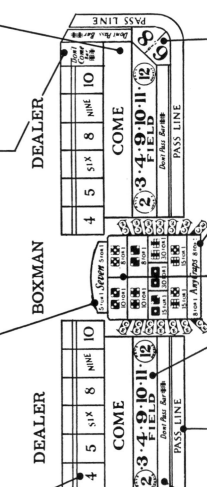

DON'T-PASS LINE

The don't-pass line is the same as the pass line except that the player is betting against the dice and everything is reversed. Players lose on a natural 7 or 11 on the first roll and win on craps 2 or 3. When 12 is rolled it's a standoff with nobody winning. If a shooter establishes a point, then makes it, the player loses. Players win if the shooter rolls 7 before making his point.

PASS LINE

On a pass-line wager, the player bets with the dice and payoff is even (1 to 1). The player wins on a natural 7 or 11 on the first roll, loses on craps, 2, 3, or 12 on the first roll. Any other number on the first roll is the shooter's point. The player wins if the point is thrown again before a 7 appears, in which case the player loses.

STICKMAN

FIELD

Bets can be made that any of the following numbers will appear: 2, 3, 4, 9, 10, 11 or 12. If 3, 4, 9, 10 or 11 show, the player will be paid even money. Player wins 2 to 1 on 2 and 12. If 5, 6, 7 or 8 show the field bets lose. This is a one-roll bet.

ODDS

When a point is made (either the shooter's point on the first roll, or a come point on a succeeding roll) a player can take the odds. A player will receive 2 to 1 on 4 and 10, 3 to 2 on 5 and 9, 6 to 5 on 6 and 8. He lays the same odds when he bets against the point.

BIG 6 or 8—Player places bet in either or both areas. Player wins if number bet is rolled before 7 comes up. It's an even money bet in Nevada, and a 7 to 6 bet in Atlantic City.

ANY CRAPS

Player bets that next roll is 2, 3 or 12 and collects 8 for 1.

This center section is bet by handing chips to dealer and stating your proposition bet. The craps and eleven bets are one-roll bets.

HARD WAYS

Player wins if the point is rolled the hard way. (Example: hard way 8 is two 4 s.) He loses if the same total number is rolled any other way except the hard way, or if 7 appears before the hard way number is rolled.

(c) Gambling Times Magazine, 1018 N. Cole Ave., Hollywood CA 90038

Diagram 1-2

few sets of dice to the shooter. That player selects a pair of dice and is ready to roll. The casino rules for throwing the dice are simply to roll them across the table so that they hit the wall at the opposite end. Other than that, any way you throw them is O.K.

After you have thrown the dice, the action proceeds as follows: If, on the first roll, you make a 7 or 11, you have shot a *natural*, and you win. What you win is the equivalent amount of chips you have bet on the *pass line*.

If you roll a 2, 3, or 12 on your first throw, that is called *craps*, and you lose. The dealer picks up your *pass line* bet. However, the shooter does not relinquish the dice. He continues to hold the dice until he *sevens out*.

If, on the first roll, you shoot a 4, 5, 6, 8, 9, or 10, that is your established *box point*. The object then is to keep rolling the dice until you make that number again. You lose, however, if you roll a 7 before making your box point.

* * *

These are the basic rules of craps. There are many other bets that can be made, all of which are explained in Diagram 1-2.

Although casinos throughout Nevada abide by the basic rules, there are some differences in odds that casinos offer players. On one-roll *field* bets for example, some casinos give 2 to 1 odds on the 2, and 3 to 1 odds on the 12. Other casinos might allow the *pass line* bettor to take double odds on the box point. If, for example, you bet $5 on the *pass line* and you rolled a 6, you would be allowed to bet $10 in back of your *pass line* bet which would pay off at $12 for your $10 *odds* bet. Now that you know the basic rules, the dealer will be happy to inform you of any house variations.

* * *

What you have just read covers the basics of craps. If you study and learn this easy-to-follow text, you will know as much about the fundamentals of craps as a pit boss, boxman or dealer. Most importantly, you will be an informed and knowledgeable player. The next step is to play like a pro and increase your chances of winning each time you step up to the craps table.

Best Betting

Once you study and become acquainted with the various kinds of wagers described in Diagram 1-2, the roll-by-roll action at the craps table will become crystal-clear to you. Study this diagram, and then take note of the following comments directly related to the betting strategy I recommend.

First of all, let's look at the bets you *should not* make. These are known as *proposition* bets, and they include all of the *hard way* bets. Here, the odds in favor of the casino are from over 9% to over 11%. These are bad bets, so don't make them; save your money for the good bets. The next bets not to make are the *one-roll* bets. These are any craps, 2, 3, or 12, and also 7 and 11. The house edge ranges from 9% to over 16%. The other *one-roll* bet is the *field*, where the odds in favor of the house are 5½%.

Get Smart

That leaves us one smart area of play. In fact, it's the only form of betting that the knowledgeable players use. We're talking about betting on the shooter. Put your bet on the *pass line*, and follow these step-by-step instructions. If you are going to bet that the dice will win, you put your chips on the *pass line* directly in front of you. You can identify that area in Diagram 1-2.

The house percentage on this bet is a mere pittance. It is less than 1½%, and it will not drain your bankroll like those other bets described. This rate is reduced even further when you take full odds in back of your *pass line* bet. The house percentage is now reduced to less than 7/10 of 1%; .666% to be exact.

Here is an example. You bet $10 on the *pass line*. The shooter rolls 5 for a number. You now bet an additional $10 in back of your *pass line* wager, which means you are taking the odds on the point number 5.

If the shooter makes his point before rolling a 7, the *pass line* wins and all bettors get paid even money on their *line* bets. In addition, your $10 *odds* bet receives a payoff of $15; that's a full odds payoff of 1½ to 1. In all, you invested $20 and you now have $45, a net profit of $25.

If you did nothing else at the craps table except play the *pass line*, take the full odds every time a point was established, and bet according to the progressive money management method I'm going to suggest, you'd be the smartest player at the table.

Some Money Management Tips

Here is our recommendation for that winning program:

(1) Increase your bets *only* on wins. Keep your bet at the same starting level after any loss.

(2) The amount of your starting bet is called one *unit*. Thus, if you bet a $5 chip, that is your unit. If you decide to start with a $10 bet, even though that would be two $5 chips, it would still be one unit. Each time you win, increase your bets in the following progression:

When you win your first bet, you get paid one unit. You now have two units—let it ride. Your second win will give you four units. Take one unit off, and bet three units. (You have now recovered your initial one-unit bet). A third win gives you six units—let it ride. The fourth win gives you 12 units—take off eight units, and let four units ride. (You now have an eight-unit net profit plus a four-unit bet on the line, all winnings.) If the next bet wins, let eight units ride so that you can reap a 12-unit net profit and still have four units in winnings on the line.

The reasoning of this system is that if a hot hand comes up, you are showing a profit without taking a risk. Once you took off the first one unit, you are betting with winnings. But in order to walk away from the table with a sizeable amount of winnings, you must bet progressively.

* * *

Remember to *never* increase your bets on a loss. Any time during the progression in which you lose your bet, go back to your one-unit bet. Remember too that the term "unit" applies to the aggregate amount of your first bet. It can be a $5 chip, or

$25, or even $10, as was illustrated in the example. There is no way to guess or predict when the dice will start making passes. But as long as you stay with your one-unit bet, you will be able to conserve your bankroll until a win cycle starts. That's why I caution you against making any of those *proposition* bets—the house edge *can* and *will* eat up your bankroll.

* * *

What you've read up to this point has discussed not only the basics of craps, but also some methods of betting. True, these methods have been confined to what we consider the best bet on the table; i.e., playing the *pass line* and playing the odds in back of your *pass line* bet each time a shooter establishes a point number. Obviously, there are many other areas in which to place a bet. Learning these various areas, and knowing what the house percentage is, will at least give you an intelligent choice of where to bet your money.

The more conversant one is with a game, and each and every aspect of that game, the more knowledgeable one becomes. In a word, *confidence* is what gives any player an edge. But confidence must be earned. You must be able to honestly say, "I can play with full confidence in my knowledge and ability."

Confronting the Casino

Although we stated that you will become an expert at the game of craps just by reading and studying this text, there is also the matter of practical experience. Let's take a tour and go through the motions of entering a casino and playing at the craps table.

The casino atmosphere is responsible for a couple of known factors, both of which are pertinent to your casino visit. As they say, here's the good news and the bad news. On the plus side, we have a beautiful, well-appointed casino. It's a pleasure to play and have fun in this adult Disneyland, which features beautiful lighting and decor, exciting activity involving good-looking people, and a general feeling of festivity.

Getting more to the point of providing a conducive atmosphere to the player, we find the following: we may enter or leave a game without noticeability. Believe me, there are some places where dealers and casino personnel may give you dirty looks if you leave the game with a bundle of winnings. If one is playing in a fashionable London casino and, again, one is fortunate enough to have won a goodly sum, leaving the table should get you a haughty (but nevertheless dirty) look.

Not so in Las Vegas, Reno, Tahoe, or anywhere in Nevada or Atlantic City. Win a bunch and the dealers and casino personnel will give you more attention than if you had lost. There are no dirty looks—in fact, it's just the opposite. Players who win big are offered the courtesy of safety deposit boxes and any other kind of security that may be requested. The reasoning is quite simple: if you're a winner, the casino wants you to receive the kind of treatment that will bring you back again.

From time to time I get questions such as, "Will the casino really let you win a lot of money?" The answer, quite simply, is that they have no control over how much you win or how much you lose! In either case, there is nothing that the casino does to bring about either situation.

Now we come to the bad news of the casino atmosphere. Believe it or not, the beautiful lights, the around-the-clock activity, and the festivity and fast-paced action can sometimes make idiots of otherwise well-oriented, clear-minded individuals. Though this is a subliminal and evasive kind of thing, it nevertheless is the enemy. In effect, it's a spell. One comes from the outside "normal" environment into an arena that is completely different from our everyday life.

Keeping Your Reservations

All of this can, should, and must be countered. I can best illustrate the detrimental aspect of getting caught up in this situation with the following true story told to me by the person involved.

This is about a player who came into Las Vegas for a one-day, one-night stay. He is a successful produce merchant who found gaming to be an enjoyable respite from his demanding business.

"I got off the plane, caught a cab, and was in the hotel just before noon," he said. "The room clerk had my reservation, but said the room wouldn't be ready until about one o'clock. Instead of having a little lunch and maybe even a drink to relax me, I checked my bag and practically ran to the craps table." Shaking his head in disbelief, he told me that in less than one hour, he dropped all the money he had during a one-hour session at the craps table.

That story was told to me after I had delivered one of my usual gaming talks at a businessmen's luncheon meeting. I do this frequently as a goodwill measure for our magazine, *Gambling Times*. I always comment on casino demeanor and how important it is to plan one's gaming sojourn so that situations like the one just mentioned can be avoided. In telling me his sad tale, that fellow vowed he would no longer put himself in such a position. He has long since learned how to pace himself, and never again succumb to any one gaming session which would destroy his entire bankroll. He learned that the exciting atmosphere alone is the biggest edge the casino has over the player.

The amount of money in your bankroll is only relative. One person comes to gamble with a stake of $200, someone else has $2000, and others play with bankrolls of $10,000 to $100,000. I repeat: it's strictly a relative situation. The person with $200 is just as anxious to turn his stake into a winning gaming holiday as the person with more money.

Taking Your Time

Granted, there's a lot of luck involved in bringing a player home with winnings, but it still remains a matter of intelligent casino demeanor. One shouldn't run over to the table and get caught in a bad streak that will eat up an entire bankroll. I suggest that as you walk into the casino, you acclimate yourself to the scene. Walk around. Become familiar with what's going on. Stand at a table and watch the game, go ahead and even make some mind bets. Those tables, those games, the action you see goes on continuously. What you will be gaining by these observations is a casual attitude and possibly a discipline that is so necessary in properly playing the games.

Naturally, each situation is different. But let's say you are in Las Vegas for the usual two-night, three-day stay. That's enough time to have some fun around the pool or enjoy other outdoor activities, attend some shows, and do some drinking, eating and people-watching. Inbetween all of these pleasurable activities, you'll have plenty of time to play your favorite games. Since the subject at hand is craps, let us approach the craps table and enter the game.

* * *

The first step is to take out the amount of money with which you wish to play. Your discipline must be such that you *will not* take out any more money in the event you lose the initial amount. By doing this, you will not suffer the possibility of losing all of your money. Our reasoning here is twofold: first, it's likely that if you weren't lucky enough to hit a win streak with your initial bankroll, then taking more money out of your pocket would be throwing good money after bad; secondly, discipline helps you spread your money out to last you through your three-day vacation.

Keeping that in mind, we suggest dividing your entire bankroll into playing 15% of it per session. Let's say you've got $500 with which to gamble over your three-day stay. That would give you $75 for this craps session. Therefore, have that amount ready when you walk up to the craps table. Give your $75 to the dealer and say "Chips, please." In all events you will receive 15 $5 chips.

Las Vegas has different stakes at different tables; some have a $2 minimum bet, others a $5 minimum bet. Don't worry about the limits—they are always ample enough. With 25 $5 chips you must play both aggressively and cautiously. By aggressive we mean just one thing: you bet progressively more on your wins. By cautious we mean you never double up or increase your bets on a previous loss. Cautious also means to place your bets in the betting arenas that give you the best odds.

Betting the Numbers

While it's true that craps is strictly a game of luck, it's also true that the winners are those players who *press* their luck. The word "press," incidentally, is a term in craps: it means to add the previous win to your bet. Here's an example. If you *placed* the number 9 for $5 and a 9 was rolled, you would win $7 in profits. The dealer lets your $5 *place* bet ride but pays the $7 in winnings to you. At that point you may say, "Press it up," in which case the dealer extracts a $5 chip and places it on top of your existing $5 bet. You take the $2 in winnings. You now have the explanation of *press* in craps. I will, however, explain the procedure of making bets on the numbers.

Once the shooter makes a comeout roll and establishes a point number, players around the table start to make bets on the numbers. This is not to be confused with *place bets*: Yet, when a bettor making *numbers* bets says "*Place* the four, five, nine and ten for five dollars each, and *place* the six and eight for six dollars each," he is using correct terminology. In that particular case, the bettor covers all of the numbers at the minimum allowable bet for a total of $32. What happens now? Every time the shooter rolls a number, that *numbers* bettor will receive the following payoffs: $9 winnings on a 4 or 10, $7 winnings on the 5 and 9, and $7 winnings on the $6 placed on the 6 and 8. Therefore, in each case, if you are going to *press* up your bet on a previous win, you know that you add $5 of your winnings on the 4, 5, 9 and 10, and $6 on the 6 and 8.

The house edge on *placing* the numbers is as follows: The true odds on a 4 and 10 would be 10 to 5; the house pays you 9 to 5. The true odds on a 5 and 9 are $7.50 to $5; you get paid $7. The true odds on a 6 or 8 are 6 to 5; the house is paying you $7 for your $6 bet. Incidentally, playing the numbers 6 and 8 is the best *numbers* bet.

The exact mathematics are as follows: When you *place* the 6 or 8 and receive odds of 7 to 6, the house edge is a hair above 1½%; when you *place* the 5 or 9 and receive 7 to 5, the house edge is exactly 4%; when you *place* the 4 or 10 and receive 9 to 5, the house edge is 6 2/3%. Now you know what's against you in the house percentage when you make those *numbers* bets.

There is a way around the higher house odds against the 4 or 10. A bettor may *buy* the 4 or 10 and receive full odds of 2 to 1 by paying a 5% fee which is called *vigorish*. For example, if you bet $100 on the 4 or 10, you actually pay $105, and if you have a win, you receive a full $200 in profits. That gives you $200 for your $105 investment, or a house edge of 4¾%.

Overall, betting the numbers is not too bad of a house percentage and gives the bettor a chance to parlay winnings if those numbers keep hitting. I can say unequivocally that you *must* increase your bets on each win if you're going to walk away from the table with winning chips. The opposite is to make what are called *flat* bets. This means, for example, you bet $5 and, win or lose, you keep betting $5; whereas in progressive betting you increase your bets and take your profits as the dice hit, if they do.

* * *

Let's see what happens to two bettors playing the numbers for the minimum of $32. One bettor is making *flat* bets, the other is making *progressive* bets, and we assume we have a decent roll going. Once the shooter establishes a point number we make our *numbers* bets. During the hand the shooter rolls a 4, which gives us a *press* up to $10 plus profits of $4. Next, in rapid order he rolls a 6 and an 8. In each case, the *numbers* bets were increased to $12 and we put two winning chips in the rack. Now a 5 and 9 were rolled and we again go up to $10 on each of those numbers, plus $4 more in winnings. The shooter now makes his *box point* number. After the *pass line* bets are paid off and the *don't pass* bets are collected, the shooter will be coming out for a new point number. At this time, we doubled all numbers that were made, which were the 4, 5, 6, 8 and 9. Our *numbers* bets now total $59.

Importantly, the house proclaims that in the comeout roll there is no action on any of the *numbers* bets. They do this because in almost all cases, the players betting the numbers are also *pass line* bettors. Therefore, if the shooter makes a 7 on his comeout roll, the *pass line* bettors win but the *numbers* bets are not disturbed. To explain further, obviously a 7 in the middle of a roll wipes out all *numbers* bets. But in this case it has become a standard agreement that only on the comeout roll there is no action of any kind on the *numbers* bets. Of course, it also means that if the shooter's comeout roll is a 4, 5, 6, 8, 9 or 10, there is no action on those numbers either. Just as an aside, all *come* bets would lose if the shooter rolled a 7 on his comeout. (We will go into *come* bets when we finish this discourse on the *numbers* bets.)

As it happened, our shooter rolled an 8 for a number. So, our *numbers* bets are back in action. He rolls a 5, which gives us a $14 payoff. Now, on our first win, we *pressed* up the amount we won, but on subsequent wins we are going to take some profits. The dealer pays you $14 for your $10 number-5 win. You take $9 and leave $5, saying, "*Press* five dollars more." The shooter rolls a 6, you get $14, take $8 in profits and *press* up another $6. He rolls a 4, which gives us an $18 payoff. Again we *press* up $5 and put $13 in profits in the rack. Now he comes back with another 5. Our $15 bet gives us $21 in profits. This time we're going to move up to $25 on number 5. We still have $11 in profits from the $21 payoff which we add to our rack.

Taking some profits and yet increasing our bets is the only way to make money on a lucky roll. Just think of it: if a 5 is rolled again, we will get a $35 winning payoff. That's $3 more than our initial $32 bet. And believe me, when the dice are making numbers this can all happen.

* * *

Let's continue with our scenario. Our lucky shooter makes his 8, which gives us a $14 payoff. We take $8 in profits and *press* number 8 up to $18. The shooter makes a comeout roll, and this time it's a 7 and all *pass line* bettors win. Back he comes with another 7 and, luckily for us, our *numbers* bets are not affected. Now the same shooter comes back with a 10 for his point number. Since this is a comeout roll, the *numbers* bets are not working. But on the next roll they are. He then rolls a 5, which does in fact give us that $35 win which we take, letting the same $25 *numbers* bets stand. Moving all bets up to the $25 level is a worthwhile goal when starting with a $5 minimum bet. We now take the $35 in profits and let the $25 bet stand. Next an 8 is rolled, which gives us a $21 payoff. We take $15 in profits and *press* up $6 to make it a $24 number 8. Our existing $10 bet on number 9 gives us a $14 payoff. We *press* up $5 and take $9 in profits. Back comes another 9. With $21 in profits, we *press* that 9 up to our $25 level, and take $11 in profits. The shooter rolls another 5, which gives us $35 more to add to our rack. And then the inevitable: up comes a 7 and we lose all bets.

* * *

Well, it was a decent roll and when we add up our winnings, we should have something to show for it. Incidentally, although we started with a $32 across-the-board *numbers* bet, we had a total of $112 left on those numbers when the shooter sevened out. However, here is what we won by making progressive bets: $164. And here is what was won by the *flat* bet player: $109. He took his profits each time the same numbers were made, and when the shooter sevened out, he still had the same $32 on the line.

Each time a number is made after you've *pressed* your bets up to the $25 mark, you are taking profits of $45 for a 4 or 10, $35 for a 5 or 9, and $28 for your $24 bet on the 6 and 8.

Craps Terminology

ANY CRAPS—A one-toss bet on all of the craps numbers with one unit, or group of units, bet on the 2, 3, 12. Payoff is 7 to 1.

ANY SEVEN—A one-toss bet on any of the possible combinations of 7. Payoff is 4 to 1.

BANKROLL—A player's total amount of betting money. Many players divide their bankrolls into smaller increments to extend their betting ability.

BARRED NUMBER—Can be either the 2 or 12. Creates a *standoff* or *push* when betting *don't pass* or *don't come*. In a standoff or push, neither you nor the casino win any money; your bet is unaffected.

BET NUMBERS ACROSS—A group of five bets on all the place numbers *other than the point number.*

BIG 6 or BIG 8—A bet made on either 6 or 8 that it will be rolled before a 7 comes up. Pays 1 to 1.

BOX POINT—Shooter's number: 4,5,6,8,9, or 10.

BOXMAN—The casino employee who supervises the craps game and deposits money into the drop-box.

BUY BET—A place bet made at true odds rather than at place odds. Carries a 5% fee.

CHOP—A term which designates dice action of win-lose, win-lose, win-lose, etc.

COME BET—An even money bet that is exactly the same as a *pass line* bet, *after* the shooter's point is established.

COMEOUT ROLL—The shooter's initial throw of the dice after a *pass line* decision.

CRAPS—Common name for the game of dice. Also the name given to the toss of 2, 3, or 12.

CRAPS/ELEVEN—The name used to indicate bets in the specially marked area on either *any craps* or *eleven.*

DON'T COME—An even money bet that the shooter *will not* toss his point again before tossing a 7. The same as *don't pass* bets, after the shooter's point is established.

DON'T PASS—An even money bet that the shooter *will not* toss his point number again before tossing a 7. The same as *don't come*, except that the shooter's point is the point number for the entire table.

DOUBLE ODDS—A bet permitted in some casinos in which the player takes an *odds bet* at twice his original wager on the line.

EASY NUMBER—Any even number that appears in any combination other than as an actual pair, e.g., 1 & 3 versus 2 & 2.

FIELD BET—A one-toss bet that 2,3,4,9,10,11 or 12 will be the next roll of the dice. (Some layouts use 5 instead of 9; some pay double or triple on either 2 or 12.)

FLAT BETS—The type of wagers in which the player bets the same amount on each roll, win or lose.

FREE ODDS—A bet on true odds permitted with *pass* and *come* bets. Unlike *buy* bets, these do not carry a 5% *vigorish* charge.

FRONT LINE—The same as *pass line.*

FULL ODDS—The correct odds.

HARD NUMBER—An even number that appears exactly as a pair. Two 2s is known as *hard four.*

HARDWAY BETS—Bets made, in a specifically marked area, on an even number, that it will appear exactly as a pair. Payoffs are for greater amounts than if the number appeared as any other combination.

HIGH/LOW—A one-toss bet on both the 2 and the 12, with two units bet. Payoff is 30 to 1 unit.

HIGH ROLLERS—Players who have relatively large amounts of money with which to play.

HORN BET—A four-unit bet that covers all three of the craps numbers (2,3,12) and also the 11.

HOT HAND—A succession of passes.

HOUSE—The casino; the management.

INSIDE BETS—A *place bet* on 5,6,8 and 9.

LAY BET—A *place bet* made that the shooter will toss a 7 before the number bet on. Player must wager more than he expects to win. A *lay bet* is a *don't place* bet at true odds.

LAY ODDS—An additional bet that allows the *don't pass* and *don't come* bettors to give, rather than take, true odds on their bets.

LAYOUT—The physical playing area in any game, usually printed on felt in the center of all tables.

NATURAL—A 7 or 11 on the comeout roll.

ODDS BET—An additional bet which can be made by players having *pass line, come, don't pass* or *don't come* bets, that the shooter will make his point. Paid at correct odds, or *full odds*.

OFF—A term indicating that bets are *not working*.

ON—A term indicating that bets *are working*.

ONE-ROLL BET—A bet decided on the next roll; as the *field*, 7, 11, or *any craps*.

OUTSIDE BETS—A *place* bet on 4,5,9 and 10.

PAIRINGS—The two numerals that come up together on a pair of dice.

PASS—A winning decision for *pass line* bettors.

PASS LINE BET—An even money bet that the shooter will make his point again, before tossing a 7. The same as a *come* bet, except that the shooter's point is the point number for the entire table.

PERCENTAGE—In gambling, the hidden or direct charge made by the casino.

PIT BOSS—The supervisor of the gaming tables.

PLACE BETS—Numbered boxes in which the player wagers that any one of the numbers 4,5,6,8,9 or 10, will come up before a 7.

POINT NUMBER—In a comeout toss, the number that is other than 2,3,7,11 or 12. That number becomes the point number for every player on *pass* or *don't pass*, and remains until a decision is tossed.

PRESS UP—To add to the bet with winnings from the previous roll.

PROPOSITION BET—A one-toss bet on any of the three available craps numbers, the 7, the 11, or *any craps* (a combination of the three craps).

ROLL—To throw the dice; a throw of the dice.

SEVEN OUT—When a shooter throws a 7 and loses, after establishing a point.

SHOOTER—The player who is currently rolling the dice.

STICK—A curved stick, which looks like a hockey stick, used by the stickman to manipulate the dice.

STICKMAN—The dealer in the center of the craps table who uses the stick to control the dice action, and the pace of the game.

TABLE LIMITS—Smallest and largest bets permitted at the table.

THREE-WAY CRAPS—A one-toss bet on each of the three craps numbers, with three units bet. Payoff is as shown on the layout *for the number tossed.*

TOSS—A single throw of the dice.

UNIT—Any fixed quantity, when used in describing types of bets or systems.

VIGORISH—A 5% fee paid on a *numbers* bet, which guarantees the player full odds on the bet.

WORKING—A term used to imply that a bet is in full force and effect, even though the entire table may not be in effect at the time. Reverse is *not working*, which implies that for a given period of time the bet is *not* in full force and effect.

WRONG BETTOR—A person wagering that the dice lose; a *don't pass line* bettor.

Chapter 2
Blackjack, or "21":
Basic Strategy and Money Management

There was a time when craps was the leading game in the casino, but today blackjack is the favorite game for both men and women. A good share of this increased popularity must be attributed to the many books and articles on the game of blackjack. Rather than being a game based strictly on chance, blackjack has a good semblance of skill attached to it.

When any game presents options for the player, the beginning of skillful decision-making moves exists. In the game of blackjack all of the options are open to the player, and none to the dealer. Therefore, it becomes a matter of the player making what should be the right decisions. Those decisions to be remembered come from case histories of situations for each of the many different types of hands that are dealt.

Here is one example. The player is dealt an ace and a 10, resulting in blackjack. The dealer's open card is an ace. The question put to the player is, "Do you wish to take *insurance?*" The answer is no. In fact, the player should never take insurance, as it is a bad bet. This simple illustration merely indicates one of the options that the player must commit to memory.

After you finish this chapter you will have learned not only the rules and playing procedures, but also the basic strategy of blackjack.

Learning Blackjack

The first step, of course, in playing any game intelligently is knowing the basic rules. It must be pointed out that these rules are *typical*, not universal. You will find slight variations in some Las Vegas casinos and in casinos in other parts of Nevada and abroad.

The player attempts to obtain a total of cards equal to or less than 21 so that his total is higher than the dealer's. If his total is higher than 21, he busts and automatically loses, even if the dealer subsequently busts as well.

Number of Players

One to seven players play against a house dealer. The players do *not* play against one another, but each plays against the dealer. Thus, other players' hands and the actions they take have no direct bearing upon your hand and your play. Nevertheless, it is advantageous to play at a table with few or no other players since it is then easier for you to keep track of the cards and, of course, you get more plays during the time you put in.

Number of Cards

The dealer uses from one to eight 52-card decks. With one or two decks, he deals by hand; with more decks, he deals from a shoe. While the rules of the game remain the same however many decks are used, you have the best advantage in single-deck play.

The Shuffle and Cut

The cards are shuffled thoroughly by the dealer and cut by one of the players, usually by inserting a joker or blank card into the pack at the place where it is to be cut. After the cut, the top card is normally *burned* (discarded) in such a way that the player cannot see its value. In multiple-deck games, after the decks are placed in the shoe, it is general practice to place the blank card about three-fourths of the way back in the pack, which signals the point at which a new shuffle is generally made.

Betting

All players place their bets in front of them, generally in a small circle or rectangle on the felt, *before* any cards are dealt. (See Diagram 2-1.) A player may play more than one hand, but must usually place twice the minimum wager on each hand, if playing two hands, and six times the minimum wager on each hand if playing three hands.

Diagram 2-1.

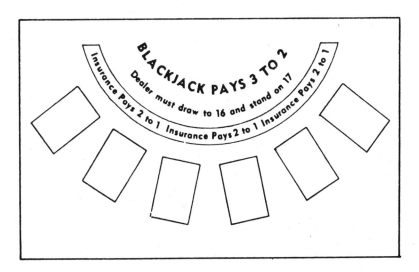

The minimum bet varies from 25 cents to $25, and the maximum from $50 to $1000. Very small gaming rooms may have a maximum bet as low as $10. Except for player's blackjack and insurance (discussed under *Player's Options*), all bets pay even money—one dollar paid for one dollar wagered. In the case of a tie, or *push*, between a player and the dealer, the bet is a standoff and no money changes hands.

The Deal

Starting at his left, the dealer gives each player a card in turn and then gives himself a card. He repeats this procedure. One of the dealer's cards is dealt face up and the other face down. The players' cards are dealt either all face up or all face down. Whether they are face up or face down makes absolutely no difference; in fact, the beginner is better off playing an up game, where he can see all the cards from the start and where other people and even the dealer might be willing to advise him.

Chapter 2

The Value of the Cards

All the picture cards—jack, queen, king—count as 10. All the other cards count as their face value except the ace, which, at the player's option, may count as one or 11. For example, if a player draws 6, 4, ace, he would clearly count his ace as 11 to make 21; on the other hand, if he drew 6, 7, ace, he would count the ace as one for a total of 14.

Soft Hands and Hard Hands

When a hand contains an ace which may be counted as 11 instead of one, without the total exceeding 21, that hand is referred to as a *soft* hand. Any other kind of hand is referred to as a *hard* hand. For example, a hand containing ace, 7, is considered to be a soft 18. A hand containing 10, 8, would be a hard 18. A hand containing ace, 7, 10, would also be a hard 18 since the ace cannot count as 11 without the total exceeding 21.

Blackjack

When the player or the dealer is dealt an ace and a 10-value card (10, jack, queen, or king) as his *first* two cards, he has a blackjack, or *natural*, which is an automatic winner. When the player receives this hand, he turns over his cards immediately; and when his turn comes, he is paid at the rate of three to two, or 1½ times his wager.

Remember, to get paid at this rate of three to two, the player must achieve 21 with his *first two cards*. All later totals of 21 pay only even money when they win. When the dealer has a natural 21 on his first two cards, he immediately collects all wagers except in the case of a player's blackjack, which is considered as a tie or push.

The Draw

Starting with the player on the dealer's left, each player may elect to *stand*—that is, draw no additional cards—or *hit, split, double down,* or *surrender* his hand. He generally signals he wants to stand (also called *staying pat* or *sticking*) by placing his cards under his wager. In face-up games, where the cards aren't touched, he indicates standing by placing his palm down on the table. A player may continue to draw cards to his hand, one at a time, by calling for a *hit* (an additional card) until he chooses to stand or until he busts with a total exceeding 21. The player generally signals a hit by scratching his cards toward him against the felt or in face-up games by scratching the felt with his finger.

When the player busts, he automatically loses his bet on that hand and must turn his cards face up immediately, at which time the dealer collects his bet and his cards. This is the *only* advantage the dealer has over a good player. That is, he wins when a player busts even if he subsequently busts as well.

The Dealer's Strategy

The dealer really employs no strategy, for his play is determined automatically by the rules of the game. If his initial hand totals 17, 18, 19, or 20, he *must* stand. After the players have drawn, he pays all hands that are higher than his, collects from all hands that are lower, and declares a tie with all hands of equal value. If the dealer has a total of 16 or less, he *must* continue to hit his hand until it totals at least 17 or until he busts. He cannot hit a hand that totals 17 or more.

Some casinos rule that the dealer must hit a soft 17—that is, ace, 6—a rule disadvantageous to the player. And should you ever come across a game where the dealer wins all ties, forget it. You are giving the house a mammoth 9% advantage.

Player's Options

In addition to drawing additional cards, the player has several options which are not available to the dealer. These are *splitting, doubling down,* taking *insurance,* and *surrendering.* It is with regard to these options that you are most likely to find variations from one locale to another and even from one casino to another.

Splitting pairs. If the player has two cards of the same denomination—that is, two aces, deuces, nines, and so on—he may choose to turn them face up and put up an amount of money equal to his original bet, playing each card as a separate hand. Ten-value cards may also be split. Some casinos require that they be of the same order—that is, two jacks, not a jack and king. Most casinos, however, consider all 10-value cards to be pairs. Except for aces, a player may draw to each new hand as often as he wishes until he decides to stand or until he busts. However, because they are such potent cards, the house allows the player only one card, dealt face down, for each of his aces.

Finally—and again with the exception of aces—if the first card the player draws to either hand after splitting is of the same denomination as the split card, in effect making another pair, he may split again and bet another amount equal to his original wager, and he may continue to do so each time he makes an additional pair.

Doubling down. When, after receiving his first two cards, a player feels he has a good hand that will become a very good hand with one additional card, he may turn his two cards face up, wager any additional amount up to his original bet, and receive one and *only one* additional card, usually dealt down. (Normally, if the hand is worth doubling at all, you should bet the full amount to which you are entitled.)

Some casinos permit doubling down only with a two-card total of 10 or 11. Others do with 9, 10, or 11, while many permit doubling down with any two-card hand. When one of the two cards is an ace, it is referred to as *soft doubling* since the player has a soft hand.

Insurance. When the dealer's *face-up* card is an ace, many casinos offer the player a side bet as to whether or not the dealer has a 10-value card in the hole—and therefore a natural and an automatic winner. Any time he has an ace showing, the dealer must offer this *insurance* bet before he looks at his hole card.

Insurance is paid at the rate of two units for one bet, and the player can bet up to one-half his original bet. If the dealer has a 10 in the hole—and hence a blackjack—the player loses his original bet (assuming he didn't also have a blackjack) and wins the insurance side bet. If the dealer does not have a 10-value in the hole, the player loses the insurance bet and continues to play his hand as he would normally. In general, insurance is not a sound wager.

Surrender. Most Nevada casinos do not have this option at present. It works as follows. When a player looks at his hand and the dealer's face-up card and decides that he has the worst of it, he may throw in his hand before drawing any other cards and surrender half of his original bet. This is an advanced play that should be ignored by beginners since it can be easily used to their disadvantage.

These then are the basic rules for playing casino blackjack. Once you have mastered them, you are ready to learn basic strategy, which is a method of deciding whether to hit, stand, double down, or split a pair on the basis of mathematical probability.

Basic strategy varies according to the number of decks in play. Because four-deck games have become so common in Las Vegas, we present in Diagram 2-2 a basic-strategy chart for four decks as developed by blackjack expert Stanley Roberts.

Diagram 2-2.

HARD STANDING STRATEGY:

Stand on...	...when the dealer's up-card is
13 or more	2, 3
12 or more	4, 5, 6
17 or more	7, 8, 9, 10, A

SOFT STANDING STRATEGY:

Stand on...	...when the dealer's up-card is
soft 18 or more	2, 3, 4, 5, 6, 7, 8
soft 19 or more	9, 10, A

You should hit any soft total less than 18 whatever the dealer's up card is.

HARD DOUBLING STRATEGY:

Double down on...	...when the dealer's up-card is
11	2, 3, 4, 5, 6, 7, 8, 9, 10
10	2, 3, 4, 5, 6, 7, 8, 9
9	3, 4, 5, 6

Never double down on a hard total of eight or less or on a hard total of twelve or more.

Diagram 2-2, continued
SOFT DOUBLING STRATEGY:

Double down on...	...when the dealer's up-card is
A,7	3, 4, 5, 6
A,6	3, 4, 5, 6
A,5 and A,4	4, 5, 6

With a soft total of nineteen or more, you should never double down but instead follow basic strategy for soft standing.

PAIR SPLITTING STRATEGY:

Never split 4,4.   Always split A,A.
Never split 5,5.   Always split 8,8.
Never split 10,10

Split the following pairs..	...when the dealer's up-card is
9, 9	2, 3, 4, 5, 6, *, 8, 9
7, 7	2, 3, 4, 5, 6, 7
6, 6	3, 4, 5, 6
3, 3	4, 5, 6, 7
2, 2	4, 5, 6, 7

* Note that you do not split 9's when the dealer's up-card is a 7.

NEVER TAKE INSURANCE

Blackjack Terminology

BASIC STRATEGY—A computer-developed method for playing blackjack—without keeping track of the cards—that may be easily memorized by a player.

BLACKJACK—A popular betting game in which the bettor is dealt two cards, either face up or face down; the dealer has one face-up and one face-down card. The object of the game is to have cards totaling 21—or as close to 21 without going over, and coming closer to 21 than the dealer. A score of 21, when dealt an ace with a 10 or a picture card, is called "blackjack."

BREAKING HAND—A hand that will *break* (go over 21) with a one-card draw, such as a hard 12,13,14,15 or 16. Also called a *stiff*.

BURNED—Discarded; what is done with the top card after the deck is cut so that the player can't see its value.

BUSTED—To overdraw to a total greater than 21; an immediate losing hand.

COUNTING—The ability of a player to keep an accurate mental record of the cards that have been played. Can allow players to have a relatively good idea of which cards remain in the shoe.

DOUBLING DOWN—An option in which the player, feeling he has a good hand which will win with one more card, turns his two cards face up and adds to his bet by as much as his original bet. This gets him *one* additional card.

DRAW—To obtain additional cards to the original two cards.

FACE CARD—King, queen, jack.

FIRST BASE—The first seat at the blackjack table, immediately to the left of the dealer.

HARD COUNT—The true face value of the cards being played with.

HARD HAND—A hand without an ace, or one with an ace that can only be counted one way (for example, an ace, 6 and 9).

HIT—To add another card to a player's hand. The player asks the dealer for another card by saying or signaling, "hit me."

HOLE CARD—The dealer's face-down card.

INSURANCE—A side bet offered to the player by the house, when the dealer's face-up card is an ace, that the dealer has a 10 as his hole card, making blackjack. Pays 2 to 1.

MONEY MANAGEMENT—The manipulation of increments of one's bankroll in betting, the better to overcome adverse house percentages.

NATURAL—A total of 21 in only two cards. Automatic winner, pays 3 to 2.

PIT BOSS—The person in charge of the blackjack games.

PRESS—To increase the size of the subsequent wager.

PUSH—A tie between the dealer and player in which no money changes hands; a standoff.

SHOE—A dealing device for multiple-deck games.

SOFT HAND—A hand with an ace which can be counted as 11; like an ace and a 7, which can be counted as totaling 8 or 18.

SPLITTING PAIRS—An option the player has with two original cards of the same denomination (4s, 8s, etc.) of splitting the two cards and playing each hand individually.

STAND—What a player does when he is satisfied with his existing cards and stays with his hand as is.

SURRENDER—The ability of the player to give up only half his bet when it is apparent that there is no way that the player can beat the dealer. Must be done before any cards are drawn. Available only in certain casinos.

THIRD BASE—Last seat at the blackjack table, immediately to the right of the dealer.

TOKE—The tip or gratuity given to dealers from players.

"21"—Another name for the game of blackjack. Also, the winning total in blackjack.

UP CARD—The dealer's face-up card.

Chapter 3
<u>Slots</u>: A New Look
at the Progressive Machines

The task of getting ahead of the progressive slot machines is not an easy one. As a matter of fact, most visitors to casinos, experienced players among them, consider the slots to be such a high risk, with a low probability of payoff, that they don't even bother with them! These much-maligned gaming devices have been nicknamed, as everyone knows, "one-armed bandits," referring to the ostensible hopelessness of any player leaving their midst in the black.

Not so fast! Although it is true that for most players—especially the inexperienced—the slots hold little opportunity for raking in a big win, in actuality there *are* ways to scientifically tackle the odds of those enigmatic spinning reels with their seemingly infinite number of combinations that can turn up on an evidently random basis. Many brilliant and determined mathematical analysts have painstakingly compiled data based on long periods of observation. They have derived formulas that help the player determine what kind of odds he is dealing with for a given jackpot, what it will take to get to that jackpot in terms of time and money and, most of all, if the payoff will be large enough to justify these expenditures.

Know Your Machine

First, let us clarify what we mean by a "Progressive Slot Machine." It is one in which the jackpot available to the winner becomes progressively larger as more and more coins are fed into the device. The jackpot increases at a fixed percentage rate of accumulation as the money is played and the lever is pulled. A win, of course, decreases the jackpot, and once some lucky devil walks away with the whole take, the pot falls back to a minimum level and begins to build again.

A Double Progressive Slot Machine (DPSM) has two such pots, usually with one jackpot substantially larger than the other. The two jackpots, as they build, are displayed in illuminated numerals atop the machine, and an arrow lights up next to the jackpot being played at that moment. This tricky little arrow switches from the larger to the smaller jackpot and back again, at the drop of every second coin into the machine. If, for example, you're playing a five-coin machine and you walk up to the machine when the arrow is illuminated on the larger jackpot, drop your first two coins in—now the arrow is on the smaller jackpot; then your next two—now it's back to the larger one; on the last coin you drop, the arrow will still be set on the larger number. See how it works? The best way to play, therefore, is to make sure that as many of your lever pulls as possible are aimed at the *larger* jackpot. The way to accomplish that—the popular 5-5-2 method of slot playing—will be explained a bit later.

The Scientific Approach

Those spinning reels with their colorful little fruit decals (oranges, cherries, plums, sevens, what-have-you) are a source of endless fascination for novice and veteran gamblers alike. An almost hypnotic effect takes place upon the player as the decals repeatedly come up in an innumerable variety of combinations. But let's look at it scientifically for a moment. Look at the chart on the machine, and determine how many kinds of decals are contained therein, which combinations pay off, and what the payoffs are. That's the easy part. Now, if you like, you can go for something a bit more complicated.

When you look at the window of the slot (see illustration), you'll notice that three rows of *fruit* are visible: on the center line (which is the payoff line), the one immediately to the top, and the one immediately to the bottom. What many experienced players do to dope out a machine is to spend a good amount of time—a couple of hours, for instance—feeding in coins and pulling the lever, meticulously noting not only which combinations come up, *but the three-decal sequence on each reel that is visible after each turn.* After several hundred pulls are made, an idea of the pattern

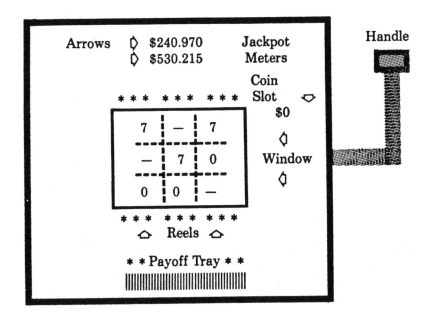

of decals on each reel can be assessed. Pocket computers, and the expertise needed to use them, can be inordinately helpful in this.

Another tricky matter is trying to determine how many decals are on each reel. Since there is invariably just one 7—the super-jackpot winning figure—on each reel, and a row of 7s is needed to win the pot, then finding out how many total decals are on each reel will give you your jackpot odds. Many canny casino players wait around for maintenance personnel to open the machine to clean or repair it, and then surreptitiously count the decals over the shoulder of said person as the work is being done.

Another way is to gauge as accurately as you can the diameter of the reel, which will, multiplied by *pi* (3.14), give you the circumference, and then look at the size and spacing (which are always pretty regular) of the decals. If not an exact figure, at least a reasonable estimate of the number of decals can be made with this method. For example, let's say you've determined from observation that your reels are about three inches in diameter. 3.14 x 3 is equal to 9.42 inches. Now, if the decals are one-quarter of an inch long, spaced about three-sixteenths of an inch apart, that means there's one decal every seven-sixteenths of an inch around the reel, a total of about 22. To utilize this method, of course, your powers of observation will have to be pretty sharp.

Staying With It

Now it's time to calculate what your chances are of Hitting The Big One, and how long (as well as how much!) it will take to get there. All kinds of frustrations can be inherent in this. There have been cases in which an intrepid coin feeder has pumped round after round of money into his trusty DPSM, waiting with satisfaction as the larger pot grew and grew, cannily playing a 5-5-2 coin pattern (more about that later) to increase his chances at the bigger take... Then, after hours of playing and much discouragement, walking away in disgust to find a more profitable machine... Only to discover that, seconds later, some innocent fool dropped in *one* handful of nickels and took off with the whole coveted pot. Ah, the injustice of it.

After many hours of playing, and innumerable handfuls of coins, playing steadily, barely stopping to eat, rest, or enjoy any entertainment... after all this energy poured into one machine, it just doesn't pay to walk away. Chances are, statistically speaking, that you're "due" to hit the jackpot fairly soon. It's like tilling a field and letting someone else reap the harvest. To cut down on the individual's stress and strain, therefore, many slot players are organized into teams. Sometimes six or more players will get together and pool a bankroll, after careful observation has pointed out a profitable machine to them. The team players then take turns playing this machine—actually monopolizing it for 24 hours a day—until one of the players hits the jackpot. This pot, of course, is then divvied up among the team members. This kind of collective playing can end up being a profitable venture for the determined gambler.

Are You Serious?

We are not talking here, you understand, about the casual, bet-for-fun player or the person who simply wanders into the casino to kill a few hours and blow 10 bucks. To study the workings of the progressive slots is the occupation of a determined and involved player. After all, the average man or woman, who is combining gambling with the rest of a restful and satisfying vacation, doesn't particularly care to spend an entire three-day Vegas jaunt pinned to one machine, passing up leisurely meals, fun, entertainment and socializing to focus on that jackpot! If you're strictly "in it for the money," though, you may find much success by watching the slots, clocking them, and doing some more calculations which we will describe later.

There are a number of factors to consider, once you decide you're serious about this, in order to evaluate your shot at the jackpot for a given DPSM. Let's go over them.

The Odds Are...

First, look at the size of the larger jackpot and the amount of the smaller take. How many reels are there—three, four, or five? How many different symbols would you say you've observed on each reel? You'll have to consider the "out-of-pocket," or net, cost of each lever pull when no jackpot is won. The kind of minor payoffs there are, as well as the rate of increase of the progressive pots, must also be noted.

Let's begin. If we know how many reels there are (obvious by simple observation) and how many symbols or decals are on each reel (possible to estimate using the methods mentioned earlier), we can figure our odds of the big win. Remember that the jackpot-winning symbol, usually a 7, is virtually always present only once on each reel—making a row of 7s, of course, the longest shot in the machine. So if, for example, there are 22 spots (decals) on each of three reels, the odds of getting three 7s lined up are 22 x 22 x 22 (or 10,648) to 1! If you think *those* odds are high, take a look at what they would be on a four-reeler: The same 22 spots on four reels would yield a 234,256:1 ratio.

Now you have to do a little more figuring. What kind of a jackpot is needed to justify going for such high odds? What kind of payoff will make this machine a profitable investment? If, in the former instance, it takes 10,648 pulls, on the average, to give you your shot at the jackpot, and you make 360 pulls an hour, that means you'd be playing for 29 hours steadily to hit that pot of gold. Only the maximum number of coins that can be played into the machine on one turn will avail you of a chance at the jackpot (if it's a five-coiner, that means only the five-coin shots will make it possible), so a substantial investment is needed.

Follow the Arrows

Let's look at the pattern by which the lit arrow switches from the larger to the smaller jackpot on a DPSM as you play. Usually, the arrow will switch after every two coins are placed in the machine, as mentioned earlier. If we play every pull with five coins, or 25 cents on a nickel machine, because of the small-large-large-small-*small,* large-large-small-small-*large* pattern that the arrow will follow, we'll end up playing an equal amount of money toward the smaller and the larger pots.

Do we really want to do this? After all, with the kind of investment we're making, we want a maximum chance at our big jackpot, at the minimum possible cost. Isn't that what it's all about? So the smart way to up our odds would be to use five coins for two pulls in succession (wait till the arrow points to a large number; then you'll have a neat large-large-small-small-*large*, large-small-small-large-*large* to give you two large shots in a row), and every third pull, put in two coins (now we're up to small-*small*) which will go, of course, toward the smaller jackpot.

You are forfeiting your shot at the smaller pot to play this way, but two-thirds of your pulls go toward the larger jackpot, as opposed to only 50%, or one-half of your pulls, going toward the large take playing 5-5-5-5 (or five coins every round). Not only that, but by playing your 5-5-2 configuration, you're cutting your total cost per pull from 25 cents to 20 cents (12 nickels, or 60 cents, every three rounds; or 20 cents a round). Over a long period of time—in which you'll invariably be playing, if you're serious about that pot of gold—a 20% cost decrease can mean you're able to play that much longer, giving you an even better shot at the Big One. So the wisdom of 5-5-2 should be readily apparent.

The Cost Per Pull

Now it's time to calculate your out-of-pocket cost per pull. This will be somewhat less than your total cost per pull (about 20 cents) since smaller payoffs along the way will neutralize some of the expenditure. To figure a general out-of-pocket cost per pull (remember, it can change with a burst of luck!), play for a fixed amount of time, noting at first how much money you've started with. Don't set aside any small payoffs, but recycle all monies back into the machine, and when the amount of time is through, determine how much of your initial bankroll is gone. Divide this figure by the approximate number of pulls made during this time (you will have clocked your individual speed on this) and you will have a good estimate of your net cost per pull on this particular machine. Different machines, of course, will yield different costs per pull, depending on their smaller-payoff rate, so a little research around the casino should point you to a device that's a good bet.

Let's say your cost per pull on a given machine works out to 12 cents. Remember the odds mentioned earlier of three-reel machines with 22 decals per reel? 10,648 to 1 was the figure, to refresh your memory. So, at 12 cents per pull, a jackpot of over $1277 would have to be offered by that machine in order to make that 30-hour play worthwhile. No one wants to spend all that time for close to even money, obviously, so a figure considerably larger than $1300 is what's required to make this a profitable venture.

* * *

That's why the size of the jackpot is so important. Watch the rate of increase of the jackpot as you play. On a DPSM, each pot increases at a 5% rate, so multiplying the smaller pot by 20 will give you the figure which is the total sum that was fed into the machine since the last jackpot. And if you divide this total by your total cost per pull, you'll know roughly how many pulls have been made since the previous big win. (These are rough estimates of course, not exact calculations.) Subtract this number from 10,648 (for a three-reeler) and you'll get an idea of how many more pulls, on the average, would yield a jackpot in this situation.

Remember, the figures you'll be coming up with are *theoretical averages*. Over a period of time, the odds prove themselves to be pretty constant. But chance, on an individual basis, always includes a "wild card" in the deck; that's why once in a blue moon, the widow from Tacoma will drop in her five nickels for a single, impossible shot at the jackpot . . . and get it. (Nearby, you can be sure, will be an experienced slot-clocker gnashing his teeth.)

Playing the 3-3-2

Now, take a look at the three-coin machines, usually three nickels or quarters. On a three-coin machine, a 3-3-2 sequence of playing the coins is more profitable than straight threes, for the same reasons delineated for the five-coin slots. You're building the bigger jackpot faster, and not wasting any time or money going for the smaller pot, which would only serve to cut your gains, cost more, and spoil your shot at the big take.

Suppose there is a row of three-coin nickel machines, we're playing 3-3-2, and the jackpots are something in the neighborhood of $550. After 10,648 pulls, one jackpot, on the average, will come up. Those pulls' out-of-pocket costs come to about $500, roughly 29 hours of playing time needed. Now, if a player were to put this $500 into the machine, including any smaller payoffs, there is a chance that the player could reach the jackpot before all 10,648 pulls are made. After all, unless he stepped up to the machine immediately after the previous jackpot was won, it stands to reason that some of these pulls will have been used up by other players.

Suppose, then, that our lucky player does hit the jackpot ahead of schedule and goes on to another machine to play. By that time, without a recent win, one of those other machines in the row will be up to a jackpot of $600 or so. Now he starts to play, returning all revenue and smaller payoffs into the machine, and by payoff time he's incurred a gain of about $100.

The Bankroll Factor

Table 3-1 illustrates the exact chances of winning a jackpot and multiple jackpots, or losing everything, with a $500 bankroll played. (Remember again, these are the theoretical averages of what happens, not precisely what will occur with you.) It turns out that 37% of the time, our player will go completely broke. But there's an equal chance that during this play he will win one jackpot, an 18% (slightly less than one in five) possibility he will get two jackpots, and an almost one in 10 (8%) chance of winning three jackpots. Now, those odds aren't terrific but they're really not all that devastating either.

Table 3-1

Event	Probability of Event	Financial Outcome
Win no jackpot	37%	Lose $500
Win 1 jackpot	37%	Win $100 or more
Win 2 jackpots	18%	Win $700 or more
Win 3 or more jackpots	8%	Win $1300 or more

In Table 3-2, we see the odds for the same play, but with a $1000 bankroll to start. Now the chances of losing it all are down to 14%, encouragingly, but the chances of winning one jackpot are down to 27%. Interestingly, the probability of winning two jackpots with this play is the same as that of winning one. The chances of winning three pots is now up to 18% from 8%, and there are smaller chances of 9% and 5% for winning four and five jackpots, or more, respectively.

Table 3-2

Event	Probability of Event	Financial Outcome
Win no jackpot	14%	Lose $1000
Win 1 jackpot	27%	Win $400 or less
Win 2 jackpots	27%	Win $700 or more
Win 3 jackpots	18%	Win $1300 or more
Win 4 jackpots	9%	Win $1900 or more
Win 5 jackpots	5%	Win $2500 or more

Now let's turn to the quarter machines. Here the stakes are really high. We approach a row of these machines, each with a $6600 or higher pot, and begin playing our 5-5-2 for the 10,648 turns needed for an average of one jackpot, requiring an initial bankroll of (hold your breath) $6000.

Imagine the same scenario we described earlier. We are feeding the entire bankroll into the machine, including smaller payoffs along the way, and we hit the jackpot a bit early. Now we move on to another machine, building that jackpot, so that by the time we win it's up to about $7000. Table 3-3 illustrates the odds for the different possibilities of outcome.

Table 3-3

Event	Probability of Event	Financial Outcome
Win no jackpot	37%	Lose $6000
Win 1 jackpot	37%	Win $1000 or more
Win 2 jackpots	18%	Win $8000 or more
Win 3 or more jackpots	8%	Win $15,000 or more

If we went through the identical steps mentioned above with a $12,000 bankroll, the probabilities would be as shown in Table 3-4.

Table 3-4

Event	Probability of Event	Financial Outcome
Win no jackpot	14%	Lose $12,000
Win 1 jackpot	27%	Lose $5000 or less
Win 2 jackpots	27%	Win $2000 or more
Win 3 jackpots	18%	Win $9000 or more
Win 4 jackpots	9%	Win $16,000 or more
Win 5 or more jackpots	5%	Win $23,000 or more

What can be gleaned from these figures is that with the progressive slots, the larger a bankroll one starts out with, the greater the chances of hitting a jackpot and making a substantial amount of money. Remember to play, most of the time, your 5-5-2 on the five-coiners and your 3-3-2 on the three-coiners, to maximize your shot at the Big One, and move on to another machine when you hit the jackpot on one.

The Human Element

You may notice that casino staff members will glance furtively at you as you make your calculations, and they may even come up to you and demand outright to know what you are doing. Be polite and stay cool as you answer all their questions; after all, there is no rule or law against making these calculations. (Don't expect any cooperation, however, if you decide you must have a peek inside the device to count the decals on each reel!)

Whereas a game like keno should only be played for short stretches, slots can only pay off—most of the time—after the long haul. Your prerequisites, therefore, are a substantial initial bankroll, lots of free time, and plenty of patience and perseverance.

Many slot players follow their hunches. That is, they'll get instinctive feelings about certain machines that seem to pay off faithfully while others appear to be duds. It never hurts to follow a strong hunch about a machine, combining intuition with mathematical know-how. After all, the odds against you are pretty high, so you need all the help you can get!

In Addition...

Here are some other ideas that you should keep in mind when tackling the slots:

(A) All full-time slot players should keep their equipment—notebook, pens, pocket computer, food containers—with them in a neat container, a heavy bag or satchel.

(B) Always keep your supply of coins concealed (except for the monies directly in front of you in the coin tray).

(C) Watch other expert players, the kind that seem to have a "nose" for a good machine. When they move on, ask if you can "inherit" their machine.

(D) Sometimes you can talk the change people into reserving a machine for you while you get some food or take a break. A generous tip will help in this regard.

(E) Most of all, enjoy yourself and concentrate on that Big Jackpot!

Slot Machine Terminology

DPSM—Double Progressive Slot Machine. A slot machine with two progressive jackpots, a larger one and a smaller one, with a lit arrow that alternates between them as coins are dropped into the machine.

DECALS—The printed pictures of fruit, 7s, and other symbols on the reels of the slot machine.

JACKPOT—The highest prize to be won with the machine; usually, to obtain the jackpot, three bars or 7s must be lined up.

ONE-ARMED BANDIT—Slang term for slot machines.

PROGRESSIVE SLOTS—The type of slot machines which features jackpots that grow larger as more coins are fed into it.

SLOTS—Common vernacular for slot machines.

Chapter 4
<u>Video Poker:</u>
Something More
Than a Slot Machine

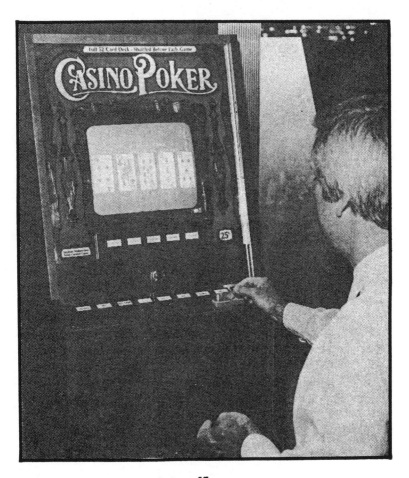

Video poker provides decision-making action for your nickels, quarters, and dollars. This automated card game closely follows the precepts of poker. For example, a royal flush is the highest hand you can get; that rare draw wins the top prize, too. A pair is the lowest hand that will win a prize. In most cases, you get your bet back if your hand winds up with a pair of jacks, queens, kings or aces. Two pairs of anything will get you a 2 for 1 payoff. Three of a kinds are worth 3 for 1. A straight, any size, wins 4 for 1. A flush nets 5 for 1 and a full house is good for 8 for 1.

Now we move up to the big time. Any four of a kind wins 25 for 1. A straight flush wins 50 for 1. And a top prize of 250 for 1 is awarded for a royal flush.

A Show of Hands

Here's a display of those hands mentioned and what each one looks like:

Any one of these picture pairs wins even money.

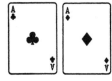

Any two pairs (regardless of size) win 3 for 1.

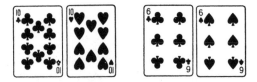

Any three of a kind wins 3 for 1.

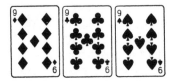

That's a straight. All five cards must be in any continuous form starting with A,2,3,4 or 5 and continuing up to 9, 10, J, Q, K, A. Any straight wins 4 for 1.

That's a flush. Any five cards of the same suit make a flush. It pays 5 for 1.

This is a full house. Any three of a kind together with any two of a kind make a full house. This pays off at 8 for 1.

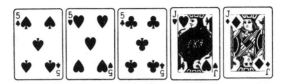

Any four of a kind wins 25 for 1.

This is a straight flush. It's the same as a straight, but all five continuous cards must be in the same suit: spades, hearts, clubs or diamonds. This hand pays 50 for 1.

The top hand—a royal flush in any suit. As you can see, this is also a straight flush, but it's the highest straight flush, 10 to the ace. You'll win 250 for 1 on this hand, plus the jackpot prize if you play five coins.

Spending and Choosing

The best video poker machines to play are those that offer a jackpot prize in addition to your regular payoff. You get this bonus when you play five coins each game.

When playing *any* slot machine you are obviously hoping to win the largest payoff the machine provides. You only get this when you play the maximum number, five coins. When you play five quarters and hit a full house, for example, your 8 for 1 odds will give you a total return of 40 quarters or a *net* win of $8.75. But when your winning hand also provides a bonus jackpot, you'll win that much more. So, always play the maximum amount, five coins, whether they be quarters or dollars.

When you drop your coins into the slot, five video windows will electronically go into motion, and then stop. What you'll see then are five cards, each randomly selected from a deck of 52 cards. This is your five-card hand and you have the option of holding any of these cards or discarding one or more. The cards you discard will be replaced by new cards which will give you your final hand.

Here is a simple example:

That's the hand you were dealt. You must now decide which cards to hold and which to discard. In this instance the obvious choice is to hold the pair of kings and discard the other three cards. You'll then be dealt three new cards which could conceivably give you one or two more kings, another pair, or even three of a kind.

The Video Difference

That hand also illustrates something else. Video poker differs from live poker in that you are not competing against other players. If this were a poker game played around a table with other players, it would be wise to hold the ace as a "kicker," discarding the 4 and 2, and drawing just two cards. That logic applies because you must beat your opponents in order to win. Drawing another ace could give you a high hand with three of a kind or even something better.

In video poker *any* size pairs—three of a kind, straights, and flushes—win, regardless of their size. But in a live game, a larger size flush or straight beats the smaller cards. A pair of aces beats a pair of kings, and so forth.

There are other differences between playing video poker and playing in a live game. There is no bluffing, no raising, and no other form of psychology used in playing video poker.

There is, however, plenty of challenge. The option of holding and discarding cards is a matter of intelligent decision. In general, it's always best to go for the higher hands. Give up a pair if you can go for a one or two card draw to an open-end straight or royal flush.

Look for the machines that pay the highest odds and the biggest progressive jackpots. And again, always play the maximum number of coins to be eligible for the jackpot bonus.

Chapter 5
<u>Roulette</u>: Learning the Wheel and the <u>Betting</u> Layout

Roulette is one of the oldest games in the casino. In fact, it is the most popular of the casino games throughout Europe. Without question it's a game of fun, and with a little knowledge and practice, it can be profitable as well. Roulette is strictly a game of chance. But, notwithstanding the element of luck involved, there are ways to play the roulette wheel that can enhance your lucky streak and enable you to win progressively larger amounts as your luck continues. In this chapter, we will discuss these methods and betting systems.

The Spinning Wheel

First, let's examine both the wheel and the betting table layout so that you can fully understand all of the bets and procedures in playing roulette.

The roulette wheel is divided into 38 numbered slots, including the numbers 1 through 36 and then a 0 and a 00. In Europe there is only a single 0, and only 37 numbered slots to the wheel. A single-0 wheel can also be found in certain selected casinos in Nevada and Atlantic City.

The house advantage is that with both 0 and 00, the player receives odds payoff of 35 to 1, rather than the true odds of 37 to 1. That house advantage amounts to 5.6% and that is how the casinos earn their money. Ostensibly they make $5.60 on every $100 wagered. The European wheel with its single 0 has a house advantage of just 2.7%; they would make $2.70 on every $100 wagered at the roulette table.

In either case, a house rake of 2.7% to a fraction over 5% is not too bad of an edge to combat. By comparison, thoroughbred race tracks take 17% to 20% for their cut.

All of the wheels in Nevada and Atlantic City have the same sequence of numbers spread around the wheel. The table layout is also the same. So, wherever you play, the rules and regulations will be familiar to you.

Getting Acquainted

Roulette is played at a table that seats six to seven players. Each player is assigned a particular colored chip which remains with that player until he or she leaves the game. Those chips must be cashed in at the roulette table—they do not have value at any other table or at the cashiers cage.

Also, each player may be playing for different stakes. The value of each player's colored chips is set by the player. If a player enters the game by asking for a stack of fifty-cent chips, the dealer will hand over a stack of 40 chips, all the same color, and receive $20; for those wishing to play with twenty-five-cent chips, a $20 bill will get them 80 chips. In order to determine the amount of each player's chips, the dealer places one of the colored chips on the rim of the wheel with a price marker on top of that chip. With up to seven players placing bets all over the table, the colored chips quickly identify each player and the dealer makes the proper payoffs quickly and efficiently.

When large amounts are won by the players, the dealer may elect to pay off with regular casino chips of $5 and $25 value. For example, if a player bet two fifty-cent chips on a single number and won, the payoff would be either 70 of the colored chips or $35 in $5 chips. If a player is winning, you'll usually see casino chips and the colored roulette chips stacked up in front of that player.

In Diagram 5-1, we see the betting table layout, with the circled letters designating each type of bet that may be made; Table 5-1 explains each of these bets and their odds payoffs.

Placing Bets

In most casinos the roulette table has a small sign stating the minimum bet per spin. It's usually a $2 minimum bet: that means $2 in accumulative bets, not one bet for $2. For example, if you're

Diagram 5–1

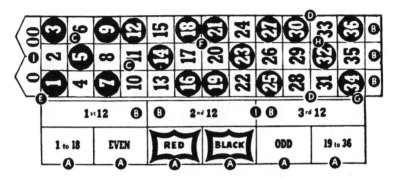

playing with fifty-cent chips you can put one chip on a single number, another chip on a two-number split bet, and two chips on red. Thus, if your single number or two-number bet loses, but the winning number was red, you'd win two chips on the red bet, and lose the other two bets if they didn't hit. In most cases you'll be betting more than four chips, so you'll make the minimum bet qualification.

The wheel has exactly 18 red numbers and 18 black numbers, with the 0 and 00 colored green. There is only one bad bet on the board: that is the "E" bet of five numbers—0, 00, 1, 2, 3. In all other bets, whether they're single-number bets, groups, red, black, dozens, columns, etc., the house edge remains at 5.6%.

After the player places his bet(s) on the betting layout, the dealer spins the wheel and then rolls the ball in the opposite direction along the top inner edge of the wheel. As the ball slows down it loses force, bounces around the slotted wheel and finally settles in one of the 38 numbered slots. That number is the declared winner.

The dealer places a marker on that particular number so that all of the players can see the results of that spin. The dealer then pays off each player who had a bet on that number or a bet on any related payoff. For example, if the winning number was 17, the following payoffs would be made:

First of all, all bets on the single number 17 would receive 35

Table 5-1

The chips used in roulette are colored for identification only. . . You set their value when you buy a stack. Using chips or coins, bets are placed on the roulette layout as shown in Diagram 5-1. There are red and black numbered squares from number one to number 36. These numbers are divided into three groups: first 12, second 12, and third 12. They are also divided for betting purposes into three horizontal groups (see the diagram) from 3 to 36, 2 to 35, and 1 to 34. Bets may also be placed on groups of numbers from 1 to 18, and 19 to 36. Also shown in the diagram are 0 and 00. These are colored green.

Betting may also be made on odd or even numbers or on red and black numbers as the dealer spins the ball. The payoff for roulette bets is as follows (see the diagram for position):

If the ball lands in. . .

A	Red or black or 1-18 or 19-36	even money
B	Groups of 12 numbers (dozens)	2 to 1
A	Odd or even	even money
B	Groups of 12 numbers (columns)	2 to 1
C	Any one number or 0 or 00	35 to 1

SPLIT BETS

D	Any one of the six in the group	5 to 1
E	0, 00, 1, 2 or 3	6 to 1
F	Any one of the four in a group	8 to 1
G	Any one of the three in a group	11 to 1
H	Any one of the two numbers	17 to 1
I	0 or 00	17 to 1

---

chips for each chip bet. Number 17 is red, which would give all red bets an even money payoff. It is also in the 1 to 18 range and a bet there gets even money. It's in the second dozen, which gives a 2 to 1 payoff, and also in the middle column, and a bet there gets paid off at 2 to 1. It's an odd-bet win too.

Betting Blocks

There's another way to select numbers and for this choice we look at the wheel in Diagram 5-2. You will note that the numbers are placed around the wheel not in 1-2-3 order, but in another manner. The red 1 is exactly opposite the black 2. The green 00 is opposite the green 0. It continues until we find black 35 opposite red 36.

Diagram 5-2

Chapter 5

Many roulette players, those who follow systems especially, play blocks of numbers as seen on the wheel. Here is an example of that method, or system, of betting.

This method requires five chips. Place one chip on a six-number bet, as shown by "D" in Diagram 5-1. Let's say you select the block of six numbers, 10 through 15. Your one chip would be placed on the line between the 10 and 13; this signifies a six-number bet covering 10, 11, 12, 13, 14, 15.

Now take four chips and place one each on 16, 17, 18 and 28. This will give you a total of 10 numbers covered with five chips. You'll notice that, as shown in Diagram 5-2, your 10 numbers are spread around the wheel so that each number is no more than three spaces apart, and in some cases only two numbered slots from each other. When the ball bounces around the wheel, it has a good chance of landing in one of the slots within the numbers you selected.

If one of your six-number group wins, you'll receive five chips to your one-chip bet. Naturally, you will lose the other four chips you bet on the single numbers. But you now have six chips, one more than the five you started with. After such a win, you should now increase your six-number bet to two chips, keeping the same bet of one chip on each of the four single numbers. If you hit one of the four numbers, you'll get a payoff of 35 chips, giving you a win of 36 chips—less the five chips invested—for a net win of 31 chips. When this happens, double all bets. If you are lucky enough to win the third time in a row, double all bets again. This is called *progressive win betting*. Remember: You *never* increase your bets on losses, but only on wins.

Take the time to read this chapter over again, so that you can become completely conversant with the game of roulette. Then plan your strategy of betting single numbers and groups so that the next time the wheel spins, you'll be playing roulette for fun as well as profit.

Roulette Terminology

BLACK—A roulette bet on all the black numbers. Pays 1 to 1.

BLOCK BETTING—The set of numbers on one section of the wheel which are bet *en masse* in certain roulette strategies.

COLUMN BET—A bet on an entire column of numbers; there are three available columns. Pays 2 to 1.

CORNER BET—A roulette four-number bet. Pays 8 to 1.

COUP—One roll; one decision. Winning bet.

DEALER—The casino employee who conducts the roulette wheel.

DOUBLE-ZERO—A bet on the 38th number on the wheel, colored green. Pays 35 to 1, as any other *straight* bet.

DOZENS BET—A bet on any of the three available groups of 12 numbers. Either 1 through 12, 13 through 24, or 25 through 36. Pays 2 to 1.

EVEN—A bet on all of the 18 even numbers. Pays 1 to 1.

GREEN NUMBERS—The zero and double-zero.

HIGH or LOW—A bet on either the first 18 numbers (Low: 1–18) or the second 18 (High: 19–36). Pays 1 to 1.

HOUSE PERCENTAGE—The advantage the casino has over the player. In American roulette, it's 5.26%.

INSIDE BET—Any bet made on numbers directly inside the layout. Odds for winning inside bets range from 5 to 1, up to 35 to 1.

LINE BET—A bet on any six adjoining numbers. Pays 5 to 1.

NEIGHBORS—The numbers immediately to the left and right of the winning number.

19–36—A bet on the second half of the numbers in the layout. Pays 1 to 1.

ODD—A bet on all of the odd numbers. Pays 1 to 1.

1–18—A bet on the first half of the numbers on the wheel. Pays 1 to 1.

OUTSIDE BET—The betting area on the roulette table bordering the numbers layout. This includes columns, dozens, black-red, odd-even, 1–18, 19–36. Pays 1 to 1.

PIT BOSS—Supervisor in charge of the roulette wheel.

PROGRESSIVE BETTING—To build up a bet by placing your winnings from the previous bet on top of your current bet.

RED—A roulette bet on all the red numbers. Pays 1 to 1.

RUN—Series of like results, such as four red or six odd.

SINGLE NUMBER—A roulette straight-up bet. Pays 35 to 1.

SIX-LINE BET—A roulette six-number bet. Pays 5 to 1.

SLOTS—Sections of the roulette wheel which hold the numbers.

SPECIAL LINE BET—A bet on the first five numbers: 0,00,1,2 and 3 *only*. Pays 6 to 1.

SPLIT BET—A bet on any two adjoining numbers. Pays 17 to 1.

SQUARE/QUARTER BET—A bet on any four numbers in a square. Pays 8 to 1.

STRAIGHT BET—A bet on any one number. Pays 35 to 1.

STREET BET—A bet on any three numbers in a line. Pays 11 to 1.

TOKE—Gratuity or tip for the dealer.

WHEEL CHECKS—The special unmarked chips that are used specifically on roulette tables.

ZERO—A bet on the 37th number on the wheel; colored green. Pays 35 to 1, as any other *straight* bet.

Chapter 6
<u>Keno</u>:
Upping
Your Chances

As any frequent visitor to Las Vegas knows, one of the most enduring and popular diversions in the Strip hotels and the downtown casinos is the game of keno. Keno is enjoyed for many reasons: It's simple to play, requires no particular skill to win big, and can be played in a leisurely fashion. Whether you're enjoying a sumptuous meal in the hotel restaurant, relaxing in the keno lounge with a cool drink, or standing in the glamorous casino lobby, you'll find the keno numbers are visible from practically anywhere in the hotel. Busy keno writers constantly make the rounds from the restaurant to the keno lounge and through the hotel lobby to dispense winnings and pick up new playing tickets. Simply put, keno is a fascinating game of chance.

The Origins of Keno

Keno today, with its automatic "goose" through which ping-pong balls printed with the keno numbers are electrically popped, is not the modern game one might assume it is. Actually, keno dates back to the Chinese Han dynasty, preceding our current version by nearly 2000 years. The game was originally introduced to the public by a man named Cheung Leung, who devised it as a way for the Chinese government to raise much-needed revenues for their army. Originally, 120 different Chinese ideograph characters were used to place bets, but this number was eventually reduced to 90. The people took to it immediately, making it a smashing success which netted loads of cash for the state. And to this day, keno has enjoyed unflagging popularity.

In the gay nineties, when Chinese immigrants brought the game with them to the United States, the 90 characters were further reduced to 80. The game soon garnered favor with Americans, who nevertheless found the Chinese ideograph characters hard to differentiate. To facilitate their play, the Chinese characters were replaced by ordinary Arabic numerals from one to 80. If you pick up a keno ticket today, you will see it is still numbered from one to 80.

A few other changes have been made. Originally, wooden balls with the keno numbers on them were pulled by hand through a wooden "goose" neck. Nowadays, lightweight ping-pong balls are used, and they are not manually moved; it's all done by machinery to ensure ease and fairness. The balls are forced aerodynamically through the "goose" and then pop up, revealing the numbers for that game. The numbers appear on an electrically lighted board in the lobby, the hotel restaurant or, for that matter, almost any place in the casino where one would get the urge to take a chance!

Originally, keno was introduced in Nevada as "race-horse keno," in which each ball popped up bearing not only a number but the name of a race horse. This "race-horse" aspect was dropped from the game in 1951, when the Nevada government passed a bill taxing off-track betting. So, for the past 31 years, it's been strictly a numbers game.

Playing the Game

While sitting in the keno lounge and sipping a drink, you can fill out a paper keno ticket for the low price of 70 cents, using the special black crayon provided, and watch the keno numbers light up on the board over the dealers' station. Although this is not the only locale in the casino where one can play, it's fun to sit in the special keno combination desk-chairs (which are a bit like the kind in old school houses, except with a convenient compartment for your drink), while cheerful, attractive keno writers are at your beck and call. This is perhaps the only big advantage keno has over the other games in the casino: it can be played in a completely relaxed atmosphere, without the dizzying adrenalin rush that so characterizes many of the table games. It's one of the reasons why keno is such a big favorite with novice bettors and recreational players.

A fascinating aspect of keno is that it is seemingly all dependent on chance, with absolutely no way for anybody to predict which numbers will surface in any given game. But there are definitely aspects of the game that you should consider before plunking down your quarters and dimes for a keno ticket. These aspects could very well give you an edge over the average, non-strategic *straight* keno bettor.

The keno ticket is played by marking off, with circles or X's, anywhere from one to 15 numbers on a ticket. The payoff on a *straight* bet will be determined by what percentage of your numbers comes up out of the ones that you bet. The minimum price of the keno ticket is usually 70 cents; a higher ticket price, of course, will get you bigger stakes. You give your ticket to the keno writer, for which you'll receive a marked-up duplicate which is stamped with the ticket number, date and game played. This is your receipt. Then, all you do is wait for your numbers to light up!

If you do win a keno game by having a number or numbers light up, you *must* present your ticket to collect your winnings—either to a keno writer or to the dealer directly—before the start of the next game. If you're too tardy in presenting your receipt, your chance to collect will be gone! So, please be prompt.

Betting... By the Numbers

If you take the time to scrutinize the payoff sheet, you'll see that the winnings really skyrocket as the proportion of the numbers chosen that come up grows. If you're playing, for example, eight spots for $1.40 and five numbers come up, that nets you a win of $12, which is a payoff of about 8 for 1. But when you're only playing five numbers, getting all five means you rake in $680—a 485 to 1 payoff—for the same ticket price!

By looking at these stakes, one might assume that it's best to play few numbers, rather than many, on a *straight* ticket. Is this necessarily so? Well, it all depends on what kind of a player you are. Remember that the house edge in the game of keno is astronomical, probably higher than that of most other games. Some players figure that, taking these high odds into consideration, they might as well play a long-shot game with just a few numbers each time, keeping their fingers crossed and hoping for a miracle. Other bettors play a high or maximum number of spots to increase their chances of having a win, and are content with a much smaller kitty. For example, if the same five spots we mentioned earlier had come up on a ticket on which 10 numbers had been played for $1.40, the payoff would have been only $2.80—not a killing, certainly, but still enough to play two or three more games and have some fun.

Ways to Play

So far, we've only discussed the *straight* ticket which, for one price, gives you one shot at one group of numbers. There is, however, a much more sophisticated way of playing keno which, for a slightly higher initial price, gives you a much better shot at picking up some winnings. This is to bet either a *way* or *combination* ticket.

With a *way* keno bet, your ticket is marked with three or more equal groups of numbers, bringing your ticket price to the number of groups times the amount you're playing; that is, playing three groups of numbers at 70 cents will cost you a total of $2.10. It is a bit more expensive to play this way, so you can't play as many games as you could if you were to just bet 70-cent *straight* tickets all night.

But remember, keno is a game which should only be played for short stretches of time anyhow, since it's impossible to buck the gigantic house edge over any length of time. And with a *way* ticket, you're much more assured of some kind of shot at a win. If, for example, you mark off three groups of four numbers, you can collect on three eight-spot bets, three four-spot bets, and the total twelve-spot bet, making the ticket price $4.90 but giving you lots of chances to win on just one ticket. Considering all the factors, it's a lot smarter to play this way than to repeatedly take your chances with a one-shot *straight* ticket. Just make sure to clearly mark, on the right-hand margin of your keno ticket, the type of bet you are taking.

Now we come to the *combination* ticket. On this type of bet, you can have groups of numbers of different count—say, two fours and a two—and bet on the different combinations. On a four, four and two-spot, one might bet on the one two-spot, both four-spots, the two different four-and-two (6) combinations, one eight-spot (the four-and-four), and also play the ticket as a total 10-spot. This gives you a great range of winnings that can come up, again, for a price of $4.90. Remember, too, that this is about the only way of playing that can give you a decent shot at the big stakes.

Compare this type of wager with the more common *straight* ticket. If you chose 12 spots, for example, on a 70-cent *straight* ticket, an eight out of 12 win would net you $150. But the same eight numerals coming up on one eight-spot *way* of a *combination* ticket will hand you a jackpot of $12,500. The smaller wins are all possible too, of course, but with the odds this high, always think in terms of a big score. Because the keno odds are so huge in favor of the house, the smart player will use his head and make each ticket really worthwhile.

The Numbers Game

Choosing which numbers to play is a personal, somewhat mystical ritual. It seems remarkable, sometimes, how certain people can invest certain numbers with a strongly directed personal force and almost "will" the numbers to appear. Many people have standard "lucky numbers" that seem to come in for them more often than not. Others will play the number of children that they have, or grandchildren, or the date of Baby's birthday, or perhaps an anniversary number.

Some canny players watch the games for a few hours without placing any bets, and write down the numbers that seem to be recurring frequently. There are two schools of thought on how to handle these commonly-seen numbers. One method is to favor these particular numbers when making your bets, since if they've been coming up regularly, there's no real reason they should stop. Perhaps there is a physical reason for this, as well: these common-show numbers may appear often because the balls holding the other numbers may be scratched or damaged in some way, and not as likely to pop up into the "goose." (But, then again, there is the theory that one should definitely play the numerals that haven't been seen in quite a while, since, according to the law of averages, they're "due" to make a showing.)

To summarize, then, the best method of playing keno is to opt for the *way* or *combination* tickets, using a pool of numbers drawn from your own personal favorites, the ones commonly seen that day, and perhaps one or two digits you haven't seen in a while. Then order a drink, relax, and get ready to win!

* * *

The following charts, illustrations, and instructions for playing keno are presented here through the courtesy of the Sands Hotel on the Strip in Las Vegas.

HOW TO PLAY

MARK SPOTS

Mark your spots' by crossing out eight numbers with a heavy X. These numbers can be chosen from any of the 80 numbers on the blank ticket. Write the price — 1.00 —in the square located at the upper right hand corner of the ticket. **Crayons and blank tickets are conveniently located throughout the club.** (Any multiple of 1.00 may be played — 5.00 — 10.00.) 2.00 minimum bet on 11 thru 15 spot tickets.

HAND TICKET IN

Give your ticket, along with the amount of your wager to any of our friendly Keno dealers. You will receive a copy of your ticket marked on an authorized copy with the next game number located in the upper right hand corner. This game number is for the next drawing of numbers. **Remember, your ticket is good for that game only!** You may use that ticket to "replay" the same numbers again on a later game; this saves you the trouble of marking a new blank.

DETERMINE YOUR CATCH

Twenty numbers of the 80 are automatically chosen. These numbers are called out over the public address system and lit on the Keno flash boards located throughout the hotel. Compare your tickets with the numbers that are lit, if five or more match the numbers you have chosen **YOU HAVE A WINNER! Present your ticket to any Keno dealer for payment before the start of the next game.** For your added convenience, special Keno tickets with the winning numbers are distributed throughout the club. Place one of these "DRAWS" with the corresponding game number over your ticket to determine the catch. **GOOD LUCK!**

it's as easy as one-two-three

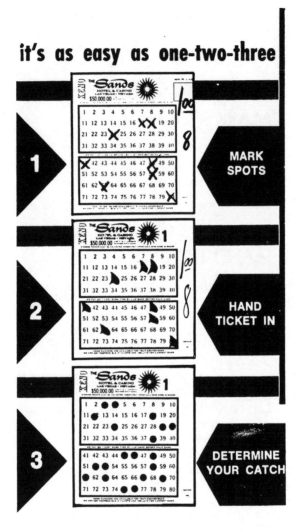

1 MARK SPOTS

2 HAND TICKET IN

3 DETERMINE YOUR CATCH

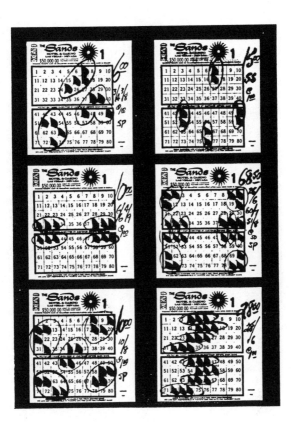

RULES

PLEASE CHECK YOUR TICKET.
Corrections must be made before start of next game or the ticket you receive will be ruled valid and accepted as issued.

KENO RUNNERS ARE FOR YOUR CONVENIENCE.
We cannot be responsible if tickets are too late for the current game.

TOTAL AGGREGATE PAYOUT PER GAME IS $50,000.00
to all players participating in the game.

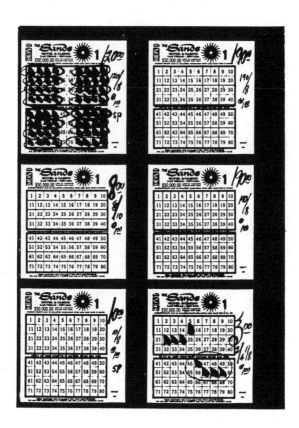

WINNING TICKETS MUST BE CASHED
immediately after each game is called and before the
start of the next game.

REMEMBER
Avoid being shut out. Play your tickets early for the next
game and also remember, you may play as many tickets
as you desire on each game... the more wagered on
each ticket, the smaller the catch needed to win the
$50,000.00 limit.

1 SPOT • Pick One Number

CATCH	BET $1.00	BET $5.00	BET $10.00
1 WIN	3.00	15.00	30.00

2 SPOTS • Pick Two Numbers

CATCH	BET $1.00	BET $5.00	BET $10.00
2 WIN	12.00	60.00	120.00

3 SPOTS • Pick Three Numbers

CATCH	BET $1.00	BET $5.00	BET $10.00
2 WIN	1.00	5.00	10.00
3 WIN	42.00	210.00	420.00

SPECIAL TICKETS NOW AVAILABLE

ON

4 SPOT THRU 9 SPOT

★ Please mark SPECIAL TICKETS ''SP'' ★

All Tickets will be paid at the regular
S1 Rate unless marked ''SPECIAL''

SPECIAL TICKETS 4 SPOT THRU 9 SPOT

4 SPOTS • Pick Four Numbers

REGULAR

CATCH	BET $1.00	BET $5.00	BET $10.00
2 WIN	1.00	5.00	10.00
3 WIN	4.00	20.00	40.00
4 WIN	112.00	560.00	1,120.00

SPECIAL*

CATCH	BET $1.00	BET $5.00	BET $10.00
3 WIN	2.00	10.00	20.00
4 WIN	200.00	1,000.00	2,000.00

5 SPOTS • Pick Five Numbers

REGULAR

CATCH	BET $1.00	BET $5.00	BET $10.00
3 WIN	2.00	10.00	20.00
4 WIN	20.00	100.00	200.00
5 WIN	480.00	2,400.00	4,800.00

SPECIAL*

CATCH	BET $1.00	BET $5.00	BET $10.00
3 WIN	1.00	5.00	10.00
4 WIN	14.00	70.00	140.00
5 WIN	700.00	3,500.00	7,000.00

REGULAR

CATCH	BET $1.00	BET $5.00	BET $10.00
3 WIN	1.00	5.00	10.00
4 WIN	4.00	20.00	40.00
5 WIN	88.00	440.00	880.00
6 WIN	1,500.00	7,500.00	15,000.00

6 SPOTS • Pick Six Numbers   SPECIAL✳

CATCH	BET $1.00	BET $5.00	BET $10.00
3 WIN	.50	2.50	5.00
4 WIN	2.50	12.50	25.00
5 WIN	90.00	450.00	900.00
6 WIN	2,270.00	11,350.00	22,700.00

REGULAR

CATCH	BET $1.00	BET $5.00	BET $10.00
4 WIN	2.00	10.00	20.00
5 WIN	24.00	120.00	240.00
6 WIN	360.00	1,800.00	3,600.00
7 WIN	5,000.00	25,000.00	**50,000.00**

7 SPOTS • Pick Seven Numbers   SPECIAL✳

CATCH	BET $1.00	BET $5.00	BET $10.00
4 WIN	1.00	5.00	10.00
5 WIN	16.00	80.00	160.00
6 WIN	420.00	2,100.00	4,200.00
7 WIN	8,200.00	41,000.00	**50,000.00**

REGULAR

CATCH	BET $1.00	BET $5.00	BET $10.00
5 WIN	9.00	45.00	90.00
6 WIN	90.00	450.00	900.00
7 WIN	1,500.00	7,500.00	15,000.00
8 WIN	19,000.00	50,000.00	50,000.00

8 SPOTS • Pick Eight Numbers SPECIAL�

CATCH	BET $1.00	BET $5.00	BET $10.00
5 WIN	5.00	25.00	50.00
6 WIN	75.00	375.00	750.00
7 WIN	2,000.00	10,000.00	20,000.00
8 WIN	25,000.00	50,000.00	50,000.00

REGULAR

CATCH	BET $1.00	BET $5.00	BET $10.00
5 WIN	4.00	20.00	40.00
6 WIN	44.00	220.00	440.00
7 WIN	300.00	1,500.00	3,000.00
8 WIN	4,000.00	20,000.00	40,000.00
9 WIN	20,000.00	50,000.00	50,000.00

9 SPOTS • Pick Nine Numbers SPECIAL✧

CATCH	BET $1.00	BET $5.00	BET $10.00
5 WIN	3.00	15.00	30.00
6 WIN	42.00	210.00	420.00
7 WIN	300.00	1,500.00	3,000.00
8 WIN	4,800.00	24,000.00	48,000.00
9 WIN	25,000.00	50,000.00	50,000.00

10 SPOTS • Pick Ten Numbers

CATCH	BET $1.00	BET $5.00	BET $10.00
5 WIN	2.00	10.00	20.00
6 WIN	20.00	100.00	200.00
7 WIN	132.00	660.00	1,320.00
8 WIN	960.00	4,800.00	9,600.00
9 WIN	3,800.00	19,000.00	38,000.00
10 WIN	25,000.00	50,000.00	50,000.00

11 SPOTS • Pick Eleven Numbers $2.00 Minimum

CATCH	BET $2.00	BET $5.00	BET $10.00
5 WIN	2.00	5.00	10.00
6 WIN	16.00	40.00	80.00
7 WIN	144.00	360.00	720.00
8 WIN	720.00	1,800.00	3,600.00
9 WIN	3,600.00	9,000.00	18,000.00
10 WIN	24.000.00	50,000.00	50,000.00
11 WIN	50,000.00	50,000.00	50,000.00

12 SPOTS • Pick Twelve Numbers $2.00 Minimum

CATCH	BET $2.00	BET $5.00	BET $10.00
6 WIN	10.00	25.00	50.00
7 WIN	64.00	160.00	320.00
8 WIN	480.00	1,200.00	2,400.00
9 WIN	1,200.00	3,000.00	6,000.00
10 WIN	3,200.00	8,000.00	16,000.00
11 WIN	24,000.00	50,000.00	50,000.00
12 WIN	50,000.00	50,000.00	50,000.00

13 SPOTS • Pick Thirteen Numbers $2.00 Minimum

CATCH	BET $2.00	BET $5.00	BET $10.00
6 WIN	2.00	5.00	10.00
7 WIN	32.00	80.00	160.00
8 WIN	160.00	400.00	800.00
9 WIN	1,440.00	3,600.00	7,200.00
10 WIN	8,000.00	20,000.00	40,000.00
11 WIN	16,000.00	40,000.00	50,000.00
12 WIN	40,000.00	50,000.00	50,000.00
13 WIN	50,000.00	50,000.00	50,000.00

14 SPOTS • Pick Fourteen Numbers $2.00 Minimum

CATCH	BET $2.00	BET $5.00	BET $10.00
6 WIN	2.00	5.00	10.00
7 WIN	20.00	50.00	100.00
8 WIN	80.00	200.00	400.00
9 WIN	640.00	1,600.00	3,200.00
10 WIN	2,000.00	5,000.00	10,000.00
11 WIN	6,400.00	16,000.00	32,000.00
12 WIN	32,000.00	50,000.00	50,000.00
13 WIN	50,000.00	50,000.00	50,000.00
14 WIN	50,000.00	50,000.00	50,000.00

Keno

15 SPOTS • Pick Fifteen Numbers $2.00 Minimum

CATCH	BET $2.00	BET $5.00	BET $10.00
7 WIN	16.00	40.00	80.00
8 WIN	56.00	140.00	280.00
9 WIN	264.00	660.00	1,320.00
10 WIN	600.00	1,500.00	3,000.00
11 WIN	5,200.00	13,000.00	26,000.00
12 WIN	16,000.00	40,000.00	50,000.00
13 WIN	50,000.00	50,000.00	50,000.00
14 WIN	50,000.00	50,000.00	50,000.00
15 WIN	50,000.00	50,000.00	50,000.00

Play Keno in our Comfortable Keno Lounge
or in the
Regency Lounge, Garden Room Casino Area and all Bars

Keno Runners — another special service —
are available at all the above locations

You will find KENO tickets available in most dining areas and lounges throughout the SANDS. Simply mark your tickets and ask any employee to have a KENO runner sent to you.

You may then sit back and enjoy yourself, watching the results on one of the many lighted KENO boards installed for your convenience.

Please remember that the KENO runner must take your ticket to the master KENO marking area to have it validated. Have your tickets ready as early as possible. We cannot accept responsibility for tickets that are turned in too late for the succeeding game.

Keno Terminology

COMBINATION TICKET—A keno ticket on which several groups of numbers are played.

GOOSE—The clear plastic apparatus through which the modern keno balls are aerodynamically propelled. In the past, the goose was made of wood.

KENO WRITERS—The people who comb the casino, collecting keno tickets and delivering winnings. The same term applies to those who write tickets behind the counter.

KING TICKET—A keno ticket on which one (king) number is used to pair up with groups of numbers.

RACE-HORSE KENO—A previously-played form of keno in which each ball was imprinted with the name of a race horse as well as a number.

STRAIGHT TICKET—A keno ticket which is played as one set of numbers.

WAY TICKET—The same as a *combination ticket*.

Chapter 7
<u>Poker</u>: The People's Choice

Poker has been, and continues to be, one of the most popular of all the social card games. Although we have other popular card games, such as bridge (which is played widely across the nation, and even abroad), gin rummy, hearts and pinochle, poker continues to be the best kind of gambling card game.

It's estimated that there are over 20 million serious-minded poker players throughout the United States. These are people who play regularly in a weekly game, usually with the same friendly group. They play at home, in social and country clubs, or in the various business service organizations.

Mapping It Out

Poker is very popular throughout the state of Nevada, where gambling is legal. There are poker rooms in most of the casinos, and various styles of the game are played. Stakes go anywhere from as small as $1 to $3 bets, up to $15 and $30, $50 and $100, and, in some places, no-limit stakes where pots may reach as high as $100,000.

California also has legalized poker; these games are played in card clubs scattered throughout the state. Some smaller card rooms have two or three tables, others have six to 10, and then there are the larger clubs. Gardena, a small Southern California municipality just 20 minutes from downtown Los Angeles, has six modern card clubs, much like the ones in the Las Vegas casinos. "The Bell Club" is also in close proximity. Located in Bell, California, a suburb of Los Angeles, this card club has more poker tables than *any* other establishment in the world. There are also a number of card clubs in San Diego and the surrounding area.

In Northern California you'll find card clubs in the San Francisco Bay area, Stockton, Palo Alto, San Jose, Sacramento, Redding, Santa Clara, and many other towns and cities.

With all the card clubs throughout the state, there is probably more card-playing going on in California than in any other state, with the exception of Nevada.

The state of Iowa has no card rooms as such. However, there are two types of social gambling licenses available: One is for beer and liquor establishments, and the other is for social and public places such as senior citizen and community centers. They have rules governing the amount of the wager permitted in their poker games. Wagers are limited to a $50 maximum; that is, no participant can win or lose more than $50 in any 24-hour period. Of course, these rules are subject to change; as time goes on, they may become more liberalized.

Oregon also has guidelines for their card clubs: No one can win or lose more than $10 in any four-hour span. These games are strictly social, but extremely popular in many places.

Montana offers municipalities the option of voting in favor of licensed card rooms. As a result, card rooms are legal in almost every city in Montana, including Billings, Bozeman, Butte, Great Falls and Helena.

The state of Washington also offers municipalities the option of voting for licensed card rooms in their areas, like Vancouver, Spokane, Seattle, Olympia and Yacama.

There is good reason to believe that with the proliferation of poker tournaments, and with more and more people playing poker, we may soon find legalized card rooms in other areas as well.

What's The Deal?

There are many different kinds of poker games. We will deal, however, with the card games played in the states mentioned.

In California, for example, only closed poker is allowed, i.e., draw poker, five cards, jacks or better, and five card lowball. The state of California, for some reason, does not allow stud poker—only draw or lowball poker. Stud poker is the game in which one gets two or three cards dealt face down, then four cards dealt up, for a six or seven card game. Five card stud is where four cards are dealt up with one card down (in the hole). Then there is the popular game of seven card stud, where there are four cards open and three down cards in your hand. There's also high-low draw, and high-low stud, which gives a win to both the high hand and the low hand. Then there is the variation, played mostly in tournaments, called Hold'em, which we will explain in detail. Lowball is a game in which the lowest hand wins. A straight of ace-2-3-4-5 is the lowest hand. Ace counts for one, and the second lowest hand is ace-2-3-4-6, then ace-2-3-5-6, and so on.

These are the most popular games played in the various card rooms and poker clubs around the country. Now here are explanations of each game, starting with draw poker.

Draw Poker

The first requirement of the game is to *ante*, which means that a previously agreed-upon amount of money is placed on the table by each player. This serves the dual purpose of giving each player an incentive to win and at the same time helps to eliminate the problem of the proverbial quitter who always folds unless he instantly draws four to a royal flush.

Next, five cards are dealt face down to each player and it is time to determine who is going to open the betting and then who is going to *call* (match the bet) or raise it. The general rule is that it takes a pair of jacks or better to open. This is when you have to exercise caution and have the necessary knowledge to make an accurate analysis of the odds. The odds depend upon how many players are involved, where you are sitting, and who opens before you. Speaking in very general terms, the odds are quite high that everyone is going to be dealt at least one pair. If you happen to have a pair of jacks, the probability that someone else has a pair of queens or kings is very high. Out of the heart of Texas comes a quote that is extremely appropriate here: "I don't open with jacks. That's gambling and my Daddy taught me never to gamble."

Chapter 7

Pay close attention to the odds. It would be an excellent idea to pick up one of the many available books on analyzing the odds and study it until you can commit most of it to memory. If you are capable of accurately understanding the odds, you will be way ahead of the opponent who goes on hunches and gut-level feelings. Their "feelings" will probably end up putting money in your pockets.

The easiest rule of thumb would be that if you are sitting directly to the left of the deal, then open with aces. If you are two seats or more from the dealer, open with nothing lower than kings. If someone in the seventh seat opens first, figure that they have at least a pair of jacks, and don't stay in the game unless you have at least a pair of queens. If you plan to raise the opening bet, then be sure that you can beat any pair. The rules on betting vary from game to game and go all the way from unlimited betting to the more common system of having a fixed amount and/or a fixed number of raises.

Now all the betting for this round has come to a halt and you are ready to draw. Again there are variations on the theme. You can "rebuild" your hand by discarding from one to five cards (the latter amount only if allowed) and getting new ones in exchange. If you have a *pat* hand, you are satisfied with the original cards dealt to you in the first place. Again there are odds to consider and, as mentioned earlier, if there is $10 in the pot and you are betting $2, then your return, if you win, will be 5 to 1. What you must consider is that if your cards indicate that the odds are 22 to 1 that you won't win, then you should not be staying in the game because the odds of winning should be better than the pot odds.

Once you know your odds and, based on the laws of probability, it appears that you have the winning hand, go for it, all the way! If you're running scared about losing your shirt, you shouldn't be in the game in the first place. Part of the battle is to come to the table armed with the proper knowledge; the other part is to back yourself up financially, without a doubt, once you're ready to make your move.

One final note: It's best not to play poker with people you've never met before. It's hard enough to "read" the expressions of people you know, let alone to come out ahead with a bunch of total strangers.

Five Card Stud

Unlike draw poker, there is only one hidden card in this game—the first one, which is dealt face down. Before the betting, one more card is dealt face up. Then after each round of betting, another card is dealt until you have five.

In this game, the main thing to look for is a pair of *anything*. A pair of twos can easily take you straight to the bank because of the limited amount of cards dealt in this game.

One of the ways to psych out your opponents is to notice if anyone keeps checking his down card. It couldn't be all that great if he can't even remember what it is!

Now, if you're hoping to pick up the fourth and or fifth card to a straight or a flush, you are treading in deep water. The only time you would stay in under these circumstances would be if no one is betting, in which case you can *check*, meaning you get a free ride this time around. In this game, if you're being stared in the face by an ace in someone else's hand, look around for other aces. If one or two others are exposed also, the chances are slim to none that anyone will get their pair.

If you've definitely got the only game in town, play somewhat cautiously. You don't want to scare everyone off by your overly bold betting. Keep everyone interested, if you can, and then grab the money and run.

Seven Card Stud

Two more cards and what do you get? Seven card stud, a most interesting game that is full of unexpected variables. Part of the intrigue is that the first two cards and the last card are dealt face down and the other four are exposed. Also, the pot gets bigger because there is an extra round of betting.

With two cards down, it is a lot more difficult to figure out what's going on in your opponents' hands. Also, there are many schools of thought on how to play this game. Some people arbitrarily stay in to get their fourth card before they decide whether to fold or not. A lot of good players stay in only if they have a pair concealed or perhaps a split pair and, of course, anything better.

The best clue to look for is this: If you are beaten on sight after four cards are dealt, it is a good time to fold your hand. Please be forewarned, though, that to stay in on a hunch or a hope is usually a losing proposition.

One rule of thumb is to pay close attention to the big bettors who *appear* to have "nothing much" going for them. It's very easy to get deceived in this game, so if you don't have the cards to play and you stay...you'll pay!

High/Low Draw

If you already know how to play draw poker, then the only change now is that the pot will be split between the high and low hands. The amateur player has a tendency to shy away from going for a high hand. Holding out for a low hand can be terribly disappointing when a one-eyed jack is staring you right in the face, especially after you have just bet your life savings during the last three betting rounds. There are two major variations: one where the players declare whether they are going for high or low or both, the other where "cards speak."

High/Low Seven Card Stud

This game has an interesting twist...you can go either high or low and, in some cases, both high and low. Since you have seven cards to rearrange any way you want, you can often set up a good low hand and then find out you have the winning high straight as well. According to one set of rules, if you are going both high and low (often known as going *pig*) and someone else has you beat for either high or low, you are completely out of the game.

Hold'em

The rules are a bit unusual because it's a seven card stud game, but you share five common cards in the middle of the table with the other players. So, with the exception of the first two cards dealt down to you, everyone has what everyone else has. Depending on how you look at it, this can be one of the most exciting or most anxiety-producing games in town. As in seven card stud, you are still looking for the best five cards. There's just enough intrigue to keep everyone on the edge of their seats. This game definitely could be subtitled "Bluffer's Paradise." The betting occurs first after each player is dealt his two hole cards; then after the first three community cards (called the *flop*) are turned over; then when each of the last two cards are individually turned (called *fourth* and *fifth street*, respectively).

Lowball

As the name implies, it is the lowest hand that wins this game. However, the rules vary on how to arrive at the winning hand. According to one set of official rules, aces are low; so therefore, a pair of aces is lower than a pair of deuces. Also, straights don't count, so the perfect low would be ace through five (often referred to as a *bicycle*). On the other hand, there is another way to play it with straights being high and, therefore, the perfect low would be ace, 2, 3, 4, and 6. . . and still a third way, called *Razz*, where the ace is high, as are straights and flushes, and the lowest hand is 2, 3, 4, 5, 7.

Poker Terminology

ANTE—To place an agreed-upon amount of money on the table before the draw. Each player bets the same amount.

BLUFF—The ability to misrepresent one's hand.

CALL—To match the previous bet.

CHECK—When the player passes on his turn.

DRAW—The basic style of poker in which each player is dealt five cards, face down, jacks or better to open.

FIVE-CARD STUD—The type of poker in which only the first card is dealt face down, and the other four are face up.

FLUSH—Any five cards, all of the same suit.

FOLD—What a player does when he tosses his cards face down, thus eliminating himself from that hand. When he folds, the player forfeits any ante or previous bets.

FOUR OF A KIND—Any four cards of the same denomination, i.e., four queens, four 9s, etc.

FULL HOUSE—A hand with three of a kind and two of a kind, of any denomination.

HIGH-LOW DRAW—Draw poker, in which the pot is split between the highest and lowest hands.

HIGH-LOW STUD—A version of poker played with seven cards, in which each player can wager an arrangement of cards as being either the highest or lowest—or playing both (called *playing pig*) a high and low arrangement.

HOLD 'EM—A variation of seven-card poker in which five common cards are shared by the players, and two cards more are held by each player individually.

JOKER—A card used as a *wild card*. In California poker clubs, the joker may be used for aces, straights and flushes only.

LOWBALL—A version of poker in which the low hand wins.

PAIR—Two of a kind.

PASS—To *not* bet.

POT—The total number of chips bet in the hand from the first bet to the final bet.

RAISE—To increase the previous bet.

ROYAL FLUSH—The 10, jack, queen, king and ace of one suit. This is poker's top hand.

SEVEN-CARD STUD—Seven-card poker, in which the first two and last card are dealt face down, and the other four are exposed.

STRAIGHT FLUSH—Five cards of the same suit in sequence.

TRIPS—Three of a kind.

WILD CARD—A card which can be used in place of any other card in the deck. This card is predetermined by house rules.

Chapter 8
Backgammon: The Basics...
and a Little More

Backgammon, one of mankind's most dearly-regarded games, has been popular for centuries. Its fascination is based on the fact that the game is actually a combination of skill and luck, with plenty of opportunity for the player with savvy to turn any roll of the dice to his advantage.

This chapter will discuss the fundamental rules of the game of backgammon, as well as the various strategies of play that can be chosen as the game develops. You will learn the meaning of the *running* game and the *back* game, and how to accomplish them. *Blots, blocks* and *builders* will also be discussed.

A Look at the Board

Backgammon is played by two people seated opposite each other at either side of a board which is divided into four sections, or *quarters*. Each quarter has six long, pointed triangles, called *points*, which each represent a numerical place on the board. Each player has 15 *stones*, or small playing discs, that are usually black for one player and white for another. In some fancy backgammon sets, the colors can be red and white, or green and white, but the toned pieces are referred to as "black" for convenience.

The player's inner table will be the quarter in which he must aim to assemble all his stones so that he can begin *bearing them off*, or moving them off the playing board. The player moves his stones from the opponent's inner table through the opponent's outer table, then into his own outer table and, finally, to his inner table. Only after all of his stones are present back in his inner table can he begin to bear off his stones. As seen in Diagram 8-1, White's inner table is on his left while his outer table is on his right; for Black, it is vice versa.

Take a moment now to study Diagram 8-1 and look at the numbered points, seeing the direction in which each player's stones will have to move in order to get ahead of his opponent.

Diagram 8-1

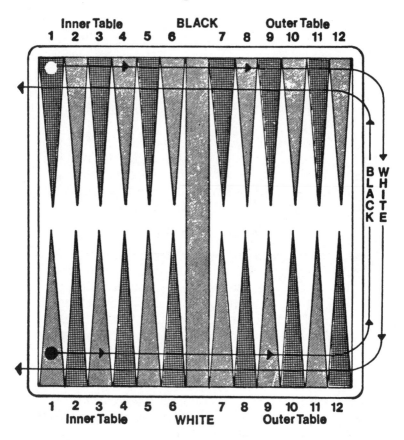

Getting Started

The next question is, how are the backgammon moves made? The players take turns rolling two dice in a dice cup. The dice are the usual kind with numbers one to six represented on each cube. Keep in mind that the two numbers coming up on the dice (for example, a 4 and 2 to make a total of 6) must be viewed and responded to one at a time, even if the player ends up moving four steps and two steps with the same stone. He can, of course, move one stone four and another two, but cannot break up the steps any other way (such as five and one or three and three). The dice must be obeyed exactly!

At the start of the game, the stones are arranged as follows: Two stones are placed on the opponent's 1-point, five on the opponent's 12-point, three on the player's own 8-point and five on his 6-point. The player's first objective is to get all of his stones *home* to his inner table; his next objective is to bear off all his stones before his opponent, and thus win the game.

A couple of rules must be kept in mind for moving the stones. One is that the stones never change direction; they cannot move backward. Also, when choosing which stone to move with the dice, it must be remembered that no player can place a stone on a point occupied by two or more of his opponent's stones. If, on the other hand, a player's throw of the dice causes him to move a stone to a point where just one of his opponent's stones is resting, he can knock out that stone and send it back *to the bar* (the center divider between the inner and outer tables), where it must wait for a suitable roll to be reentered to the game. Such a single stone is called a *blot*. Two or more of the opponent's stones on a point is referred to as a *block*.

A player always uses his full throw (that is, the numbers on both dice) to move whenever possible. Toward the climax of the game, when more and more of the points might contain blocks for him and he finds it impossible to utilize the entire roll, he uses the large number if possible. Barring that, he will use the smaller dice if he must. But if he finds there is no way for him to use either number on the dice to make a move, he forfeits his turn to his opponent.

A double number rolled on the dice is fortunate, because it also doubles the player's roll. In other words, a 4 and 4 thrown actually become 4 and 4 and 4 and 4, which can be used on anywhere from one to four different stones to advance them. On doubles, two stones can be moved together, if desired, establishing a new block for the player on a fresh point.

Needless to say, it is strategic to attempt to move a stone onto a point where one or more of your own stones already are. To move a lone stone onto a new point deems it a blot, and vulnerable to attack by your rival. As in many other things, when it comes to moving your stones, there's safety in numbers.

Also remember that when a blot of yours is hit and sent to the bar by your rival, you must use your next roll to reenter that stone. If, because of blocks, you cannot reenter your blot with the numbers you've rolled, then you are stymied; you can't move until such time as you can come up with a roll that makes this possible. So, avoid unprotected stones!

As always, there's an exception to this rule. In some cases, strategic players will take a calculated risk on a blot, because for them it is the first step in establishing a block; in other words, the first lone stone is a *builder* that will later be joined by another stone, if possible, on the following roll. But this is always a risky maneuver and the odds should be weighed carefully before proceeding with it.

Things to Remember

The *priorities* of backgammon should always be kept in the player's mind. First priority: Getting all stones into the inner table. Next priority: Bearing them off. But also important are: forming blocks to stymie your opponent's progress, hitting blots to send to the bar, and avoiding blots yourself. Every roll of the dice should be used to implement these objectives, preferably more than one objective at a time.

If a player manages to bear off all his stones before his opponent, he wins the game. But a double win is provided if he can manage this feat before his player has borne off even one stone. Then the win is called a *gammon.* Even better than a gammon is a *backgammon,* in which a player accomplishes the bearing off of all his stones while the opponent still has one or more stones in the winner's inner table, or at the bar. This type of win is equivalent to winning three games!

There are a couple of rules to remember about bearing off. As mentioned before, no stone can be borne off until all the player's stones are present in his own inner table. Also, an exact roll is needed to move the stone off the board. In other words, if Black has a stone on his own 4-point, only a roll of 4 would permit its exit from the board. On a six, a die with 6 is needed, or a 4 and 2, to exit the stone, and so forth.

At each roll of the dice, the player should mentally run through all possible moves made available by the roll, and try to go for the one that will serve the most different objectives. Merely advancing a stone forward is not enough. The player should advance forward into a block, move another piece to hit the opponent's blot, or set up a *prime* (six blocks adjacently held); in this way, accomplishing not only his own progress, but the hindrance of the advancement of his opponent.

Whether one plays a *blocking game* (in which one concentrates mainly on blocking the opponent's progress toward bearing off), or a *running game* (in which the main objective is rushing to bear off one's own stones), depends heavily on how the game shapes up after the first few rolls. Backgammon is one game in which the player who starts the game (determined by the initial roll) has a heavy advantage. At the start of the game, each player rolls a single dice, and the one with the higher number starts the game. His starting roll is the combination of his number and his opponent's. If they tie, they must roll again, until one of the players has a higher figure. This one starting roll can give a player a clear edge that is difficult to cancel out.

Let's Play

Let's say White gets to go first and rolls a wonderful 6-5, which allows him to advance from 1B to 7B, and from 12B to 8W. Then Black rolls a 6-4. This allows him to, if he wishes, move one of his *runners*, or black stones, from 1W to 7W, so building his *bar point*; but isn't it more strategic, in terms of the aims mentioned above, to use his 6 to go from 12W to 7B, hitting White's blot and sending it to the bar, and take his 4 as a move from 12B to 9B, where White would need a total of 8 to hurt it? This isn't all that likely, so it would be a safe move. All Black would have to worry about, in this instance, is the possibility that White would roll a 7 or 8 combination, hitting one of these two temporary blots. Provided this doesn't happen, Black could use his next turn to double up on those blots.

The above example is, admittedly, a risky one, because it does leave Black with two blots, on 7B and 8B, for the time being. But it is always better to combine an advancing move with a *hit* of your opponent's blot, than to merely make an innocuous move that does you some good but does your opponent no harm.

On his next roll, White gets a 5 and 4. He can use the 5 to reenter from the bar, and make his 5-point by joining this stone with the one left on 1B. This powerful block is an effective retaliation for your hit.

Always remember the principle of combining your own advancement with your opponent's effective deterrent. Then you will be on your way to winning backgammon.

Playing Options

Sometimes, if you have a series of low rolls working against you, and your opponent seems to be zipping ahead with several high numbers in a row, you might consider adopting a *back game* strategy. The back game, or defensive-type game, is one in which you concentrate mainly on forming blocks in strategic places to deter your opponent's progress, and hitting as many of his blots as possible to stymie him.

By using four and six back men to make two or three points in your opponent's inner table, effectively blocking his bearing off, you are spoiling many of his rolls; by sending his blots to the bar, you can effectively clear the way for some of your runners to make it into your own inner table. As one well known backgammon connoisseur, Professor Hoffmann, points out, no one should begin a game of backgammon with the intent of playing a back game, but any player must be prepared to deal with the necessity of playing one should it arise.

The bearing-off stage of backgammon, where all the strategy

begins to pay off, can be very tricky. One must play a smart game when bringing one's stones into the inner table by not crowding them all on one or two low numbers; this quickly makes the odds against bearing them off impossibly high. Remember to keep a well-distributed board, with all (or most) points of the inner table effectively covered. This will ensure that a wide range of numbers coming up on the dice can be used to bear off, rather than just one or two low numbers which can be difficult to throw.

Acey-Deucy

You've just read a summary of rules and tips for basic backgammon. There is, however, a form of the game known as *acey-deucy*. This originated in America during World War II, and is being rediscovered of late. In acey-deucy, the same routes for black and white stones are followed, with the exception that there is no opening arrangement of stones on the board; the game begins with all four tables clear, and the players enter their stones onto the board according to the roll of the dice, with no restrictions for entering and moving. If a player rolls a 1–2, it is called an *acey-deucy*, and entitles him not only to that number of moves, but also gives him the privilege of chosing any double roll he wishes, laying it down, and moving his stones accordingly. Additionally, he is given an extra roll of the dice before his turn is through.

As an example, if Black starts the game by rolling a 1–2, he can open with one man on 1W and another on 2W. He could then choose double-six to play, putting an additional two men on 6W and then moving them to 12W. Then, on his second roll, if he came up with 4–3, he could move a man from 1W to 5W and another from 2W to 5W, making a block.

Of course, in the beginning stages of the game, the 1–2 roller would do well to maximize his luck by choosing a double-six for maximum progress. As the game goes on, however, and blocks abound, he may be forced to go with a lower double, else forfeit not only this shot but his bonus roll as well.

A good strategy in acey-deucy would be to get half your men

together on the board as soon as possible, since you have no ready-made blocks to begin with the way you do in regular backgammon. A player in this version of the game should try to form blocks with his runners as early in the game as he can.

An important difference between acey-deucy and regular backgammon is that whereas in regular backgammon, a blot that is hit must be reentered before any other men can be moved, the same is not true of acey-deucy. In the latter version, a man that is *hit* can be reentered at any time.

Chouette

Another version of backgammon, called *chouette*, involves one player, called the *man in the box*, pitted against a team. This player is determined by the high roller of the dice. The second-highest roller becomes the captain of the team, and makes all the movement decisions for his team, after consulting the other players. If the man in the box wins, he collects from the other team and stays *in the box* for another game, and the captain goes to the bottom of the team, with the other players moving up a place and a new captain taking over. If the man in the box loses, he pays off each player and goes to the foot of the team, while the captain becomes the man in the box and the players move up, with the previous second-ranking player taking over.

The Doubling Cube

When playing a *doubling game* (in which the stakes are doubled), serious players keep track of how the doubling stands by using a *doubling cube*—a special cube which has the numbers 2,4,8,16,32 and 64 engraved on different sides. Whoever makes the first double brings the cube to his end of the table and lays it with the 2 side upward. If his opponent later redoubles, it goes to the opponent's end and he turns the 4 side upward. This continues as long as redoubles are proposed and accepted. If declined, the final doubler wins and collects.

Backgammon Terminology

ACE-POINT—Another word for the 1-point position.

ACEY-DEUCY—A roll of 1-2 on the dice. It also refers to a form of backgammon in which this roll gives the player a choice of doubles and another roll.

AUTOMATIC DOUBLE—This is a rule which when implemented doubles the stakes if each player rolls the same number (i.e., making a double roll) at the beginning of the game.

BACK GAME—This is one in which a player might purposely set up blots, which are hit and sent to the bar, so he can reenter them to form blocks in his opponent's inner table.

BACKGAMMON—A game in which the winner scores three times the value of a single game by bearing off all of his stones before his opponent bears off even one, and while there is still one of his rival's stones on the winner's inner table or the bar.

BACK MAN—A stone on the opponent's inner table. The game opens with two *back men* on the opponent's 1-point; back men are also any stones reentered from the bar.

BACKWARD GAME—This is the act of keeping *back men* in your opponent's inner table to prevent him from bearing off, thus paralyzing his game. This technique is useful in offsetting a losing game.

BAR—The divider where stones are sent (blots) when they are hit. The bar runs lengthwise between the inner and outer tables.

BAR POINT—A player's 7-point location, the first point in his outer table.

BEARING OFF—Moving stones from one's own inner table off the board; the last stage in winning the game. Bearing off can only be done when all the player's stones are home in his own inner table, and then only on exact rolls for exit.

BLOCK—Two or more stones placed on a single point, which prohibits the opponent's stones from landing there.

BLOCKING GAME—A game in which the focus is on forming a series of blocks to impede the other player's advance.

BLOT—A single stone on one point. It is vulnerable because it can be hit by the rival's stone and sent to the bar, stopping the player's game until he can reenter it.

BOARD—The backgammon playing board; also can be used instead of table, as in *inner board* for *inner table,* etc.

BONUS ROLL—Another roll of the dice granted to a player who rolls a 1-2 in the version of the game known as acey-deucy.

BOX—As in *man in the box,* the position of the one player who takes on the entire team in the chouette version of backgammon.

BUILDER—A blot or extra stone, placed in a position where it *makes a point* or helps establish a block.

CAPTAIN—The head of a team of players in chouette who play the *man in the box.*

CATCHERS—Stones that a player has distributed throughout his board to, he hopes, catch his rival's runners and send them to the bar. This technique is often used in back games.

CHOUETTE—In this type of backgammon, a lone player, or *man in the box,* takes on an entire team of opposition, headed by a captain.

COMFORT STATION—A nickname for the opponent's 12-point. It is thus named because the player, having started the game with this point made, can stop his runners off there on the way to his own side of the board.

COVERING—The act of making a point occupied by a blot, by moving another stone to that point, thus covering the blot.

CUP—Short for dice cup.

DICE—Two cubes, with the six sides of each numbered from one to six with dots, which are rolled or thrown to determine the number of moves one makes on the board.

DICE CUP—A special cup from which the dice are rolled in backgammon.

DOUBLE—To increase the stakes in backgammon to double the original amount.

DOUBLE GAME—Another term for a *gammon.*

DOUBLES—A roll of the dice in which both dice come up with the same number, as in 3-3. Doubles give the player twice as much point value to move as is shown.

DOUBLING CUBE—A special cube—usually marked with 2, 4, 8, 16, 32, 64—which players use alternately to double the stakes.

DOUBLING GAME—A modern version of the game in which a player may, according to the regulations, double the stakes during the course of play.

ENTER—To bring in a stone from the bar to the opponent's home board

FORWARD GAME—A favorable game, or *aggressive* game, in which a player uses his favorable rolls to move stones quickly without taking unnecessary risks.

GAME—To bear off all stones before your opponent can do the same.

GAMMON—A game in which the winner scores twice the value of one game by bearing off all his stones before his opponent can bear off even one.

HIT—To move a stone to a point occupied by your opponent's blot and send it to the bar. A win of regular backgammon is sometimes called a *hit* as well.

HOME BOARD—Sometimes the player's inner table is referred to by this term.

HOYLE COUNT—The traditional way of determining which player has the lead. The player counts any stone on his 1-point as having a value of one; on his 2-point, a value of two; and so forth up to his 6-point. Then he counts how many points are needed to bring all of his stones to his 6-point. He then calculates his opponent's stones in the same way; the one with the smaller total is the leading player.

IDEAL ROLL—A 6–1 combination on an opening throw; some say 3–1 is also ideal.

INNER TABLE—The section of the backgammon board that includes points 1 to 6. This is divided into Black's inner table and White's inner table.

IN THE BOX—A term used in chouette, as in *man in the box*, to describe the player who is opposing the entire team.

KEY POINTS—Points preferred to be made as soon as possible in the game, usually the player's own 5-point, or his opponent's 5-point; followed by the bar point (7-point), and a player's own 4-point.

KNOCK OFF—To hit the opponent's block and send it to the bar. This term is used in acey-deucy.

LOVER'S LEAP—An opening or early move from the opponent's 1-point to his 12-point, as a result of a lucky 6–5 roll of the dice.

MAKE A POINT—To place two or more stones on a point, thus creating an effective block to your opponent.

MEN—Stones.

ODDS—The various chances involving hits, bearing off, and other possibilities of the game; also the probabilities of various rolls of the dice.

OUTER TABLE—The section of the board from points 7 to 12. This is subdivided into Black's outer table and White's outer table.

PLAYING SAFE—Moving stones to points already made by your other stones, rather than letting them sit alone as blots.

POINT—Any of the 24 long triangles on which the stones sit on their way to bearing off. The term also applies to a triangle that has been *made* by placing two or more stones on it so the opponent cannot land there.

POINT COUNT—See Hoyle's Count.

PRIME—Six adjacent points made with blocks and held by one player, forming a barrier his opponent can't pass.

RAIL—Another term for the bar.

REENTERING—Bringing stones back from the bar.

RUNNER—A back man which a player hopes to bring from his rival's inner table by running it past any blocks the rival may have set up.

RUNNING GAME—Similar to a forward game. It becomes a full-fledged running game when a player gets all his stones past his opponent's blocks, running them all to his own inner table and bearing them off quickly.

SPLITTING RUNNERS—To move one runner ahead of its companion.

STONE—One of 15 playing pieces, or discs, used in backgammon.

TABLE—A section of the backgammon board.

TAKING OFF—Same as bearing off.

THROW—A roll of the dice, especially when using the dice cup.

THROW OFF—To bear off or take off.

TRIC TRAC or TRICK TRACK—Old name for backgammon.

TRIPLE GAME—A backgammon win in which one has borne off all his stones while his opponent still has not borne off any, and still has stones in his own (the winner's) inner table, or at the bar.

WALKING A PRIME—To move a prime of six blocks along the board by moving stones from the back toward the front to replace others that have moved forward. A very effective method of play when it can be accomplished.

Chapter 9
Gin Rummy:
How to Play
Gin and Win

An Introduction to the Game

It would be easy to presume that gin rummy is merely a game of luck. After all, only the Fates decide what kind of a hand you get, right? But that's not the whole story. Obviously, if you have a ragtag hand of unmatchables and your opponent's is studded with aces and lined-up royalty...the odds are naturally against your walking away with the pot. But by being a clever player, you can maximize whatever assets you have, keep a sharp eye on the discard pile, and cut your losses to a minimum.

Gin rummy is played with an ordinary 52-card deck. The king is the highest card, the ace is the lowest. Picture cards count 10; all other cards count their numerical face value, including the ace which is 1. The deck is cut, and the player with the low card deals. The players are dealt 10 cards apiece alternately (two players at a time), and the twenty-first card is turned up and placed next to the remainder of the deck. The first player has the option of adding this exposed card to his hand and discarding one; or turning over a new card from the deck, keeping that and discarding one card; or discarding the new card and keeping his hand as is. The players continue in this manner until one player has gin and exposes his hand, or a player announces he is *knocking*, or exiting, the game with an unmelded value of 10 or less.

The mechanics of *melding* are widely known but worth reviewing. Three of a kind, or three or more sequential cards of the same suit, constitute *meld* possibilities. An entirely *melded* hand is *gin* and terminates the round. The game continues until one player reaches a total score of 100 points (in some locales, gin rummy is played until a winning score of 500 is reached).

127

Chapter 9

Knowing the Score

The scoring in gin rummy works as follows. The *knocker*, or the first player to exit the game with an *unmelded* total of 10 or under, collects the points totaled from the unmelded cards of his opponent. This is called a *box* or *line* score. Keep in mind that the player who *knocks* only wins the box score if his unmelded count is less than that of his opponent. If he knocks with a value of say, 8, and his opponent's unmelded value is only 6, the opponent wins the box score, which in this case will be the difference between the knocker's and his own (in this case, 2) plus a 25-point bonus. If the opponent and the knocker tie in their unmelded values, the opponent wins the hand, scoring 25 points.

Before the score is totaled, the opponent of the knocker may add any of his own unmelded cards to the knocker's melds, if he can, thus cancelling out those points. Unmatched cards equal to the knocking count (usually 10) are also discarded. The remainder of his cards are added to the knocker's score.

In the event of *gin*, the winner collects the points of his opponent's unmelded cards, none of which may be added to his melds. That and a 25-point bonus constitutes his score for the hand.

When the game is over, the final scoring is tallied by giving each player an additional 10 points for each box, and giving the winner the difference in points between his score and his opponent's. Additionally, the winner receives 100 extra points for winning the game. In the case of a *schneider*—a player who reaches 100 points without permitting his opponent to score at all—the winner receives double-point value for everything, including box scores and the game bonus.

(In the version called "Oklahoma Gin," the knocking value is determined by the value of the twenty-first card turned up. If the card is an ace, there is no knocking and the game is for *gin*.)

The Best Strategy For Winning

Most players of gin rummy automatically assume that they should play for *gin*, as this is the way to win big. But, looking at it from a purely mathematical standpoint, *gin* is the long-shot of the game and you'd be better off playing to knock! Rather than holding on to high cards in the hopes that you will be able to meld them and achieve *gin*, you're much better off reducing the numerical count of your hand as quickly as possible so that you can knock. The deck should be viewed—as well as your hand—as to its *knocking* possibilities for you, not its *gin* possibilities. Remember to knock as soon as you can, because it's dollars to doughnuts that if you don't, your opponent will! Be very careful with the cards you throw off. If you have even an inkling that your opponent needs a certain card, by all means keep it and readjust your strategy accordingly. *NEVER* throw out a card your opponent can use: this is the sure way to be a loser at gin rummy.

The discard pile is very important—watch it carefully. With a little good sense, the discard pile will map out for you your opponent's *gin* strategy and help you determine how to play your own hand.

When analyzing your hand, remember to always give more credence to the low cards, as they will do you far more good than the high ones. Don't hold on to high pairs hoping for a meld which may never happen, and don't pass up card after card with a value of four or under. This will get you nowhere. Your opponent may very well knock or *gin* first, and you will be sunk to the tune of those high unmelded cards! Cards with a value of six or more, therefore, should only be picked up when they *immediately* make you a meld. Otherwise, forget it—they're too much of a risk in the long run.

Playing Wisely

In terms of concealing your own strategy from your opponent, it is obviously preferable to choose the card from the deck (which your opponent has not seen) than to pick up the one he has just discarded. Even if you have a very poor hand, you're getting desperate, and the latest cast-off will make you a pair, look at it this way: A pair is still not a meld, and if you hold a slew of unmatched cards, the hidden card may provide you with a pair as well, without letting your opponent know where you're at. Even if it doesn't, it could be a low card which will help you knock faster. Only open cards which will form immediate melds (*not* meld possibilities, such as pairs) should be picked up.

Keep in mind that your goal is to knock as quickly as possible. Therefore, a high card or an open card which will allow you to knock immediately upon your discard should, of course, be picked up! There are exceptions to every rule.

Watch the open cards, and when your opponent picks one up, do your best to discern his strategy. If, for example, you've noticed a 7 of diamonds in the discard pile, you've got the 9 of diamonds, and your opponent takes the 8 of diamonds when it comes up, it's a cinch he's melding 8s. But what if the other player picks up the 4 of clubs when you've got the 3 of clubs and the 4 of hearts? He could be melding 4s or 4-5-6-ing it. In this case, you'd better hold on to both cards—no real hardship in this instance because they are low cards. Even if the value were high, however, it would be preferable to hold on to them, despite their knocking risk, than to throw out one of them and take the greater, more punitive risk of handing your opponent the game.

* * *

Always think this way about discards—not just in terms of what the discard will do for your own hand, but in terms of what it *could* do for your opponent's. Once you're sure your opponent needs a card for a meld, it is imperative that you keep this card even if said card puts you in a temporary deadlock. There are ways around the deadlock by slightly altering your strategy... but there's no way around handing your opponent another meld! Even if the card is a total "foreigner" to your own hand and doesn't fit in anywhere, it pays to sacrifice a pair—even a low pair—to keep it. In fact, if the number value hasn't yet been played (or consecutives) and you don't need it, the chances are more than good your opponent does! Or else why hasn't it appeared before?

This is particularly true when you are well into the game. Don't feel too badly about keeping a *non-ginning* card; you may be able to throw it off later when your opponent is well into another tack. Or you can discard it when you knock; or if your opponent knocks first, you might be able to lay it off on a meld of his.

Always try to knock early in the game: this will greatly increase your chances of catching your opponent with many high, unmatched cards to add to your score. If you can't knock by the tenth card or so, it's time to play for *gin*. This is because well into the game, your opponent has a good chance of knowing pretty much what your melds are, especially if you've picked a lot of open cards. He could probably lay off a lot of unmatched cards on your melds should you decide to knock. So even if *gin* is a long-shot for you toward the end of the game, it's better to wait for *him* to knock, and use lay-offs for self-defense, getting your knocking count below his.

Once you decide to play for *gin*, remember not to make two four-card melds. Pairs don't work, so that will force you to complete two melds to *gin* instead of just one. If, for example, you hold a 10-J-Q-K of clubs, an 8 of clubs, 8 of hearts and 8 of spades, a pair of 3s, and a 4, it would be silly to pick up an 8 of diamonds and discard the 4 if one of the 3s and the 4 were the same suit. You don't need the 8 of diamonds, and by holding on to the 4 you double your chances of achieving *gin*.

Make A Note...

To summarize, try to remember these points in the game of gin rummy:

(1) Your first priority should be to *knock*, not hold out for *gin*.
(2) Knock early in the game.
(3) Favor low cards over high ones, in general.
(4) Do your best to keep cards your opponent needs.
(5) Pick up only those high cards that will immediately meld.
(6) Pay attention to the discard pile; watch it constantly.
(7) Pick only open cards that immediately *meld*, not merely *pair.*

(8) Always try to keep both cards when you're not sure which one will help the other player.

(9) If you can't knock by the tenth discard, play for *gin*.

(10) Avoid making two four-card melds.

Follow these rules, and you will be well on your way to establishing a reputation as the "gin whiz" of your set.

Gin Rummy Terminology

BOX SCORE—The points a player makes by knocking and receiving the point value of all of his opponent's unmelded cards.

GIN—The way to win the game of gin rummy: having all 10 cards melded.

KNOCK, KNOCKING—The way a player can score the round by getting his unmelded cards' point value down to 10 or under; in this way, he gains the points of his opponent's unmelded cards.

LINE SCORE—The same as the *box score.*

MELD—To combine three or more cards either of the same denomination or same suit in sequence. A group of three or more such cards.

OKLAHOMA GIN—In this variation of the game, the knocking card—or the one whose value determines the point value under which a player must bring his unmelded cards in order to knock—is the first card of the deck turned up. If an ace is turned up, there is no knocking and the game is strictly for gin.

SCHNEIDER—What is achieved when a player reaches a total score of 100 points—whether by knocking or ginning—before his opponent can score even once. This feat doubles his score.

Chapter 10
Money Management:
A Method for Winning More and Losing Less

Money management is definitely an integral part of casino gaming. Whichever table games you're playing (craps, blackjack, baccarat, roulette), it is necessary to do two things: limit your losses and magnify your wins. This objective can be accomplished through proper money management. It's a simple thing to come by, and in this chapter we're going to tell you about money management and how it can help you to win more money and limit your losses, giving you a much nicer vacation wherever you may go for gaming fun and excitement.

Self-Control is the Key

To start with, the term "money management" has to do with the control of your bets so that, on one hand, you reduce the loss risk to a stipulated amount, but on the winning side, there are no restrictions. Yes, it's the perfect method of betting. It can account for winning more money when your luck is good, when the dice are rolling well, when blackjack is hitting... whatever the game may be. On the other hand, when you're not winning, you will learn through money management how to conserve your bankroll.

Money management, in a word, is a form of *discipline.* Your money management starts to work almost immediately upon arriving at your gaming site. As soon as you walk into the hotel, it's a matter of not rushing to put a dollar in a slot machine, $5 on the craps table, $1 on the spin of a roulette wheel... or whatever the amount, or whatever the game. The idea in money management is that you *plan* your forays into the various table games. All of this, incidentally, simply adds to the pleasure, the fun, and the excitement at your favorite game, as well as your winning potential. So, tne first thing you do upon checking into the hotel is to divide your bankroll into certain amounts. For example, let's say that you are there for a two-day stay, and during your stay you're obviously going to play at the tables, dine, see some shows, and enjoy various forms of entertainment. The difference between winning and losing money is sometimes definitely affected by how well you're enjoying your holiday.

A Betting Exercise

Let's say you're playing with $400 over a period of two days. You're going to divide that $400 into four sessions on one day and four sessions on another day. Four hundred is divided into eight equal parts to start; if you win money, things can change, as you will see. So you wind up with $50 per session. A session means you take that $50, walk over to the craps (or roulette, etc.) table, and that is the money you're going to gamble with during that playing session. The playing session ends when you walk away from the table, having lost that $50. If, on the other hand, you walk away with chips to cash in, that also ends that playing session.

Now you go to the table, hand the dealer $50 at a $5 minimum table, and get 10 $5 chips back for our cash money. If you refer back to our section on how to play winning craps, you'll know how to do what we suggested. But let's say you put $5 on the line, the shooter rolls a point, and you play $5 back on the line because you want to get your full odds, and after a few rolls you've lost $10. Well, the next shooter comes up and, in many cases, people will start to double up at this point, figuring, "Well, I lost the last time, so I'm gonna try ten dollars this time, and see if I can recoup my lost money." Well, that's wrong. In money management, and this is one of the strictest rules, you never double up on a previous loss. You do not increase your bet in any way on a previous loss.

So, according to our procedure, you place another $5 bet, and if again the shooter rolls a 4, you've got $5 in back of the line. Remember, when you're betting the line, you always take the odds in back, because that brings the percentage way down. Your *pass line* bets always pay even money. Your *odds* bets, which can be the equivalent of the amount of money on the *pass line*, can give you higher odds and bigger winnings.

Lo and behold, let's say the shooter rolls another 7 and you've lost. You're now $20 out. Again, you are faced with the temptation of doubling up to win. But that's not how it works. There's no such thing as hunches, lucky feelings, etc.; they just don't work at the craps table.

Again, after your second loss, you put $5 on the line. Now the shooter rolls, up comes a 7, and you win $5. This is your first win, and according to our procedure, we always double the amount of the bet on our first win. So this time, after the dealer pays you $5, you double up and $10 go on the line. The next roll produces an 11, and you win again. Now you've got another $10 that you're paid off, so you've got $20. Our rule calls for taking one chip back—$5. (We always use the term *unit:* betting one unit—and when you win, you bet two units.) In this case our unit has been $5, but it could be $25 as well. Now you have three units riding on the line.

* * *

Now the shooter comes out with a 6 for a number. As we mentioned, you should always take the odds in back of your bet. So, you take $15 and put it in back of your $15 *line* bet. The roller rolls a couple of more times and then makes the 6. You now get paid $15 on the line which gives you six units there, and for your $15 *odds* bet which was in back of your $15 *line* bet you get paid $18—six dollars for each five. So now you pick up the $18, together with your $15 *odds* bet, but you let the $30 ride on the *pass line* because of, as we will show you after we finish this section, the method of doubling up called "progressive betting." You bet one, win; bet two, win; take one down and bet three. Now when you make your three bet, you have six, and we leave the six to ride. This is important because this is your biggest bet so far. The shooter comes out and shoots a 7. He makes a natural 7, and you've just won another $30 (or six units). Now the rule tells us that we bet four units and take down two units in net profits. So, out of your $60 you now have $60 going, you've won $30, and have twelve $5 units. So you're taking $40 back (eight units) and letting four units ride.

Chapter 10

Your net profit off your *line* bets is now $40. In addition to the $18 won previously, you're now $58 ahead, minus the $20 loss, so you're actually $38 ahead.

Now let's say the shooter rolls a 9. You've got a $20 *pass line* bet, you take $20 and put it in back of your $20 *line* bet. The shooter rolls a few more numbers and then he comes back with a 9. You get paid $20 on the *line* giving you nine units or $40, and you get 30 to 20 on your odds bet, so you get $30 there, and you put this in your rack along with your $20 *odds* bet.

So, you're off to a good score, which continues like this. Any time you win on one unit, you bet two. Take your four units and take one down, betting three. Three units win on the line, you have six, you bet, you win and you have 12, you take down eight, you have four going.

* * *

Now the reason for this method of betting, instead of doubling-up on top of the other, is that we do not know in a chance game like craps or roulette if the next throw of the dice or turn of the wheel will give us a winner or loser. So if we hit on a "lucky streak," like the last hand, we don't know if it will continue. Never count on a lucky streak continuing, because you never can tell just when it will end. Every time another win comes, sure, it adds to the lucky streak. But you must always talk about a streak like this in retrospect, not trying to project it into the future, because we can not predict the future. So, make the most of your wins but use common sense. Leave enough on to take advantage of another win if you're lucky, but take something back in the event that you lose, so you still have some safe profits from the previous wins.

Let's say that on the next roll the shooter rolls a crap, ace-deuce. This is a loss, so you take back five units and play the original one unit, $5. Once you get a loss, you cannot make the same size bet or add anything. If you're wiped out on your *pass line* bet, you start all over with one unit. Same method: if that wins, you bet two; if that wins, you bet three; if that wins, you bet six; bet wins, you bet 4; wins, bet 5. You just keep repeating that form.

In this way, you are minimizing the amount you can lose and maximizing your wins while safeguarding them at the same time. So here you are back to our single $5 one-unit bet. Now he shoots an 8, and you take five and put it in back of the 8, and the shooter rolls a 7, so you've lost the $5 *line* bet and the $5 odds in back; so when the next shooter comes up you put $5 on the line again. But you will see that if you count up, you're still ahead this way in spite of a few losses, because you have used this progressive betting system.

Remember: The formula is, bet 1, win; bet 2, win; bet 3, win; bet 6, win; bet 4 and take back 8. (See Diagram 10-1.) Conversely, if you had taken the $50 and lost it all, you would walk away knowing you have three other $50 playing sessions.

The Progressive Money Management System

Bet in units. A unit should be a one-chip denomination, such as $1, $5, $25. Conceivably, though, if you wanted your unit bets to be larger than $1 but not as much as $5, your unit bet could be $2 (two $1 chips). For the purpose of the chart, we're going to use $5 chips as our units, as we did in the previous example.

This time we will play our progressive money management method at the *roulette* table. Here you have a choice of betting even money situations and also areas in which you receive 2 to 1 for a winning wager. Each spin of the wheel gives you a win or lose decision. (You may wish to review Chapter 5 to refresh your memory of the roulette rules and table layout.)

* * *

According to the odds of roulette as it is played in the casinos of Nevada and Atlantic City, there are 38 selections around the wheel in which to bet. They are the numbers 1 through 36, 0 and 00. As stated, there are 38 slots identical in size and space around the wheel. The true probability of selecting one of these numbers is 1 in 38, or odds of 37 to 1. However, the casino needs a little edge and they pay 35 to 1. You put a $1 chip on a number and if it comes up on that spin of the wheel you get 35 to 1, or a total of $36. That gives the house a $5\frac{1}{4}\%$ edge, which is not the worst bet in the world; you pay 17% at the thoroughbred race tracks.

If you were to make 10,000 $1 bets on an even money bet such as red or black, and if the wheel showed an equal number of red as black, you'd lose $525 at the end of the 10,000 spins. The green 0 and 00 is the house edge, and they would show up just enough for you to lose 5 ¼ % of your bankroll.

Of course, it's not likely that you'd see *exactly* 525 green numbers during any designated 10,000 roulette spins. But the house edge is a reality, and making flat bets (all the same denomination) will eventually whittle your bankroll down to nothing.

Therefore, if you are to win, you must bet progressively. Diagram 10-1 further explains and illustrates our progressive money management system. The betting formula is 1-2-3*-6-4**-8. (Bets are $5 units.)

Diagram 10-1

	Units Bet	Win	Lose	Cumulative Win-Loss
	1	1		+ 1
	2		2	− 1
start over	1		1	− 2
start over	1	1		− 1
	2	2		+ 1
* take 1 unit back	3	3		+ 4
let 6 ride	6	6		+ 10
* * take 8, let 4 ride	4		4	+ 6
start over; next bet is	1			

You advance your bets, making them progressively larger, when you win. But always go back to the original one-unit bet when a loss occurs. The idea of taking some profits off during the win sequence is one that ensures you will show some net profit on any win sequence. You continue to progressively advance your bets with each previous win.

The two-unit win bet gives you four units. However, you drag one unit, which was your original starting bet. You play the three units, and if it wins, let it ride. Then, when that wins, you take off eight units in profit, letting four units ride. The next bet would be the full eight units, and with a win there, you can move up to a 10-unit bet, dragging six units in profit.

In other words, if a really hot hand is unfolding, you want to be on it with progressively higher bets, yet taking profits along the way.

Putting Some Aside

When do you know if it's time to leave the crap table? Here is the rule: As soon as you have accumulated double your bankroll, put your original bankroll (say it's $50) off to one side of your chip rack, *where it's not to be touched again!* Now you're playing with the $50 in profits. You're using the money management plan that helped you win the $50 in the first place.

Suppose you get lucky and win another $50 with your $50 profits. You take another $50 and put it aside as you did with your original bankroll. This is just like putting it in your pocket. Each time you win another $50, you put it on the side or in your pocket to take with you. There is no way you can lose that money once it's put aside. If you ever lose the money that's in front of you, do not dip into your previous winnings to attempt to recoup. Leave that money alone once it's been put aside.

This philosophy tells us that as long as we continue to win back our original bankroll, we can continue to play in this session. This way, you can combine the thrill of winning with the security of knowing you won't walk away from the table a loser no matter what happens in your subsequent wagering. Most players don't have a method or formula like this to guide them. When they do win, they're good candidates for losing it all. This can't happen to you as long as you stick to this formula, because the temptation to pile chips on a winning bet without restraint is counteracted. In games of chance, remember that our "winning streak" or lucky cycle is only as good as the last win.

The beautiful part of this method of progressive betting is that for as long as you can gather those increments of $50 each time and put $50 in your pocket, you can continue to play in that session.

Once you get far enough ahead, you might want to take the risk of doubling up a whole roll, because you're only risking profits—some of them, not all. So whether you win or lose big on that particular roll, remember that you're still ahead of the game and you're protecting yourself.

Remember the Guidelines

Your goal is to keep building those $50 increments, and whenever you can do that, keep playing that session. Incidentally, you can always trade in $5 chips for $25 chips, or "green chips," to save space in your pocket or your rack. You leave the table when you lose the playing money in front of you. You *never* dip back into your previous wins in your pocket or the side of your rack to take out money once you've lost the amount in your current play. This way, you can walk away from the table a winner even if you've just lost all the money in your playing increment. You hope this won't happen, of course, but the idea is that even if it does, you can still walk away with the feeling of being "home free."

Once you're playing, the progressive system is working out beautifully, and you're beginning to amass some impressive winnings, you can switch from $5 units to $25 units. In that case, you've got to go in with about $200, eight $25 chips, but *the same rules apply.* You're just moving up in the world! Using these principles, you can go from winning hundreds to winning thousands. But—it's worth repeating: *stick to the principles set forth here. Never* increase your bets on a previous loss. *Always* increase your bets on a previous win (only with winning chips that the dealer has paid you). The same principles work for the Wheel of Fortune, baccarat, or any game of chance. Don't forget to use these principles in all eight playing sessions.

Remember that this philosophy—as well as your own discipline in adhering to it—will serve you well in any game of chance, at any betting level. Good luck, and win big!

Chapter 11
Gaming Tournaments:
Learning the Rules and Requirements

Casino-sponsored gaming tournaments are relatively new on the gambling scene, be they in Vegas, Reno, Tahoe or Atlantic City. For the longest time, visitors came to these resorts mainly to play the usual casino games. But now the hotels have a lot of competition with each other, and must tempt visitors with something new. Thus, tournaments came into being.

Poker

Actually, for the past ten years, there *have* been poker tournaments, the most notable being the World Series of Poker sponsored by Binion's Horseshoe Casino in downtown Las Vegas. Today this is a million-dollar tournament in which all kinds of poker games are played over a period of about four weeks. They start off with smaller pots like $25 to $100,000, moving all the way up to a $1 million game. This has brought in many crack poker players from all over the country, because the contestants get a good break when they enter the tournaments. It's very festive, attracts a lot of spectators, and the sponsoring hotel is giving something to the tournaments. For example, in Binion's all the entry fees go into the pot to be won by the players. In some cases the entry fee is $10,000. Binion's is profiting only from the publicity they will receive by sponsoring the tournament and providing the arena for this impressive contest.

The other well known tournament, the Amarillo Slim Super Bowl of Poker conducted at the Sahara Tahoe casino-resort, is much like Binion's. There are many other smaller poker tournaments going on throughout the year, attracting the most skillful players from every state and even from other countries such as England, Ireland, and France.

For the astute player, or for the player who feels he is a bit beyond average (the best, perhaps, in his own group at home), these tournaments are a real boon. In such tournaments sometimes even amateur players can walk away with a lot of money.

Blackjack

In the past five years, one casino game that has become a very popular tournament game is blackjack, or "21." This game is particularly big with younger gamblers, people in their 20s and 30s, who've learned that there is a way of playing blackjack, a certain strategy involved, which makes it somewhat a game of skill. In tournaments the players compete with each other, as well as with the house (as in roulette, craps, etc.). Here's how it works.

First of all, there are time limits on the tournaments (or a fixed number of hands to be played: 100) as well as restrictions on how much money is used. You will be eliminated from the competition or the round if and when you lose the original amount which you have bought in for. You cannot replenish losses with fresh money; once the initial amount is lost—whether it be $500, $700, or whatever—the player is out.

The time limit is usually two hours to a playing session in a blackjack tournament. In two hours you can't really put together any great playing technique, especially when you're playing against the house and your fellow contestants at the table. So, luck and timing prevail in these tournaments.

"Anyone 21 years or older can enter the $35,000 Sands International Blackjack Open. A registration fee and buy-in of $600 will be required of each contestant."

Thus reads the entry guidelines of the Sands International Blackjack Open. The players, seated together at random, are required to bet each hand with a minimum bet of five dollars and a maximum bet of $500. Even if someone has amassed chips totaling two or three thousand dollars, the limit that person could bet would still be $500.

* * *

The object is to beat the dealer *and* the other players seated around the table. There is one winner per table; the player who wins Round 1 at the table advances to Round 2. The players who lose Round 1 are out of the game, unless—and this is a recent amendment—they wish to pay another registration fee and begin again. The winner is not required to pay any additional fee. There are sometimes prizes awarded to the winners of the round.

Round 2 continues much as Round 1, with the same betting limits and rules. Players must keep their chips visible to the other players. At the end of the two-hour play, the person with the most chips is declared the winner. (In the Sands competition, exactly 100 hands are dealt, which amounts to about two hours, and a break in-between.) In the Sands tournament, a maximum of six players are seated at a table.

At the end of a round, each player gets to keep the chips in front of him or her. So even if the other five players at the table are deemed losers of the round, they may still be ahead if they each finish with more than $600, which was the entry fee. At the end of the round, the chips are cashed in, because they are not good for any other game in the casino.

At the end of Round 3, the winners are in what is called the Championship Playoff, and eligible to win as much as $75,000 in cash. That winner will be awarded the title of Sands International Blackjack Open Champion. A beautiful trophy goes along with this award, as well as a considerable amount of prestige.

The winners of Rounds 1, 2 and 3 receive bonus prizes of $25,000, $40,000 and $60,000 respectively, and nine runner-up prizes are awarded. These include complimentary accommodations in the Sands Hotel in either Vegas, Tahoe or Puerto Rico. Also, the player who accumulates the highest number of total winnings in all three rounds is awarded the title of Cumulative Winner and automatically advances to the Championship Playoff. Even if this player did not win any preliminary round, if his *total* winnings in all three rounds are higher than anybody else's, he wins the privilege of playing in the championship round.

Staying Informed

Anyone with an eye toward the big jackpot of a tournament should send away to the appropriate hotel or sponsoring casino for a rules brochure and read it over carefully. The rules are fairly easy to understand and therefore these tournaments attract a wide variety of people from all over; they provide an excellent opportunity to meet people in an exciting, high-rolling atmosphere.

These tournaments provide a great deal of fun and excitement for the few days of their duration, and provide a lot of opportunity for players to win money and prizes. In the Sands Contest last year, the Cumulative Winner was awarded a 1982 Cadillac. There are many other exciting tournaments in addition to the Sands', including those held at the Sahara, Riviera, and Tropicana hotels. By reading publications such as *Gambling Times* magazine, one can keep abreast of the various tournaments, rules and dates.

Craps

Craps tournaments are also very popular these days. The entrants are required to post a $250 entry fee, some of which is funneled into the prize pots.

Again, the table assignments for each player are randomly selected, with each player given an arbitrary number. The craps game is played the conventional way (see Chapter 1) with 12 to 14 players assigned to each table. There is one round per hour. When the hour is up, whoever has the dice—the shooter—may finish his roll. The round does not end until that particular shoot is through.

Players must keep their chips in front of them, by denomination, in their racks. As in the blackjack tournaments, the minimum bet on a roll is $5, and the maximum is $500. On the proposition bets (like hard way 4, hard way 6, hard way 8 and hard way 10), 7, ace, ace-deuce, and 11, there is a $25 limit. On all other bets the limit is $500.

As in the blackjack tourneys, whoever wins Round 1 advances to Round 2. In some places, both the winner and the runner-up at each table may advance to the second round. Each player is given a receipt for his chips, which is cashed in at the end of the round. There are cash prizes awarded along the way to the winners of each round, as in the card tournaments.

Simple rules apply to the players: Keep your chips in view,

hands off the table, etc. Courtesy and fair play are the name of the game.

Other Tournaments

Another popular contest is the backgammon tournament. The Dunes runs a backgammon tournament which has been very successful for many years. This is a glamorous, exciting game well-loved by the international jet set. Timely information as to these tournament schedules can be obtained by writing to *Gambling Times* magazine.

Gin rummy is also played in tournaments nowadays, even though it is not a casino game, and enthusiasts of the game come from all over the country to play.

* * *

The gaming tournaments, aside from providing fun and excitement for the players, also serve to promote the hotels and casinos that host them. They help to bring new faces to the scene, people who will return at a later date for another vacation.

Wherever you decide to play, remember to obtain the schedule and rules well in advance, enter as early as possible, have fun, and, hopefully, good luck!

Chapter 12
Casino Gaming:
Other Games

This concluding chapter illustrates and explains the basics of two games not covered in this book in greater detail: Baccarat and the Wheel of Fortune.

When found in casinos, these games are usually few in number and receive the least amount of player participation, although baccarat is played for high stakes and usually represents significant swings in overall casino wins and losses.

The Basics of Baccarat

Simple and Elegant

The word "baccarat" is derived from the Italian *baccara*, which means zero. The term refers to the face cards and the 10, all of which have zero value in the game of baccarat. In Europe, baccarat and a similar version called *chemin de fer* are among the most popular casino games.

Since baccarat's inception in Nevada, the game has assumed a glamour look. In most casinos, baccarat is played in a separate, roped-off area. The intention was to attract the high roller, or the more sophisticated, moneyed player. With the tuxedo-clad dealers, there is an elegance and aloofness to the game.

* * *

However, for all its enchantment, baccarat is primarily a simplistic game. There are no decisions or options: no degree of skill is required for either player or dealer. Players may sit in any open seat at the table; seating position does not affect the play in any manner. Each seat corresponds to a number on the layout, 1 through 15. Three dealers service the table. The dealer standing between positions 1 and 15 is known as the *caller*. He runs the game as cards are dealt from the shoe.

Each player gets a turn to handle the shoe. The player must bet the bank when he has the shoe, but any player may decline the shoe and it passes right along from player to player. Again, there is no advantage or disadvantage in dealing the cards; it's merely a formality and part of the ambience that players enjoy.

The caller receives the cards from the player with the shoe, places them in the appropriate boxes, and then calls for another card, or declares the winner, according to the rigid rules of the game.

Betting

Players bet by placing their chips in the numbered box opposite their seat. Bets may be made on the player or bank, and both are paid off at even money. In most games, bets range from $20 minimum to $2000 maximum.

After the winner is announced, the two other dealers at the table pay off the winning bets and collect from the losers. If the *bank* was the winner, players who won must pay a 5% commission on their winnings. Thus, if a player had a $100 bet on the bank and it won, $5 would be owed to the house.

Rather than collect this vigorish after each game, a record of what is owed by each player is kept in a numbered box just opposite where the two payoff dealers sit. Players pay this accumulated amount after the finish of a *shoe*. Each time the shoe is depleted of cards, all eight decks are thoroughly shuffled and replaced in the shoe.

Determining the Value of the Hands

All cards, ace through 9, are valued according to their count. Tens and face cards count as zero. Thus, if the first two cards dealt are a king and a 4, the count is 4. An 8 and 6, although totaling 14, would come to 4 after subtracting 10. Here is a list of two-card and three-card totals to further illustrate the method of counting cards:

Cards	Hand Total
6, 5	1
4, 10	4
3, queen	3
8, 2	0
10, jack	0
9, king	9
8, 8	6
6, 4, 8	8
10, 4, 3	7
5, 2	7

When any two cards total over a 10 count, 10 must be subtracted. The remaining total is the card count.

Rules of Play

These rules apply in all American casinos. Printed copies of these rules are available wherever baccarat is played. Dealers act according to these rules without consulting players at the table. The rules are automatic. The'highest total any baccarat hand can have is 9. A two-card total of 9 is called a *natural* and cannot lose. An 8 is the second best hand and is also called a natural. If both player and bank are dealt identical hands, it's a *standoff* (a tie) and neither bank nor player wins.

No further cards can be drawn to a two-card draw of 6 or 7.

When holding other two-card totals, player and bank draw another card at the direction of the dealer who does the calling. In studying the printed chart, one can easily determine the rules of the game.

It's a matter of letting the dealer do the calling, and declaring the outcome. Players are concerned only with how much they wager on each hand, and whether they bet on the player's side, or the banker's. The house edge in baccarat is the lowest of any casino game. With only a 5% commission on winning bank bets, and nothing taken from winning player bets, the player's disadvantage is only 1.37%. In some casinos, ties are permitted to be bet on. The payoff is 8 to 1. It's a bad bet for the player as the house edge is 14.1%.

Mini-Baccarat

A number of casinos have installed smaller baccarat tables, usually in among the blackjack tables. It's the same game, but the rituals of passing the shoe, etc., are missing, and the game is staffed by one dealer. The layout, however, conforms to the regular baccarat table, and each seat position (1 through 6) corresponds to a numbered betting box. Limits are usually from a $2 to $5 minimum up to $500 maximum. Mini-baccarat is played fast, but the exact same rules apply as in the larger game.

RULES:

Player	When first two cards total:
1-2-3-4-5-10	Draws a card
6-7	Stands
8-9	Natural-Stands

Banker — **When first two cards total:**

Having:	Draws when Player's third card is:	Does not draw when Player's third card is:
3	1-2-3-4-5-6-7-9-10	8
4	2-3-4-5-6-7	1-8-9-10
5	4-5-6-7	1-2-3-8-9-10
6	6-7	1-2-3-4-5-8-9-10
7	STANDS	
8-9	NATURAL—STANDS	

Baccarat Terminology

BANKER—The dealer hand in baccarat.

BANKER HAND—A bet that the hand called *banker* will come closer to 9 than the hand called *player*. Pays 1 to 1. A 5% fee is charged to all winning banker hands.

NATURAL—An 8 or 9 count in baccarat.

PLAYER—The player hand in baccarat.

PLAYER HAND—A bet that the hand called *player* will come closer to 9 than the hand called *banker*. Pays 1 to 1, with no commission charge.

PUSH—When hands tie in baccarat.

SHILL—A player employed by the casino who is usually at the baccarat table to help create the illusion of activity on an otherwise quiet table.

TALLY SHEETS—Slips of lined paper which enable players to keep a record of how hands are falling, and determine whether they are winning or losing.

TIE—A bet that both the banker and player hands will tie. Pays 8 to 1. All bets on banker or player are considered a push in the event of a tie.

The Basics of
the Wheel of Fortune

The Wheel

The game is known as the Big Six, or the Wheel of Fortune. It's another easy-to-play casino attraction, reminiscent of the old carnival wheels.

The wheel itself is made of wood in an elaborate and colorful design. Approximately six feet in diameter, the wheel is divided into nine parts, each part consisting of six identically spaced slots. There are exactly 54 of these slots separated by metal studs.

Positioned at the top of the wheel is a leather flap, and when the wheel is turning, a tick, tick, tick sound is heard as the strap hits against the nail-like metal studs.

Finally, as the wheel slows down, the strap will settle in one slot, and that particular one out of 54 slots will be declared the winner.

Betting

The slots are divided as follows: 23 $1 slots; 15 $2 slots; eight $5 slots; four $10 slots; two $20 slots and two slots that are joker or casino design slots.

Each of the slots carries the design of American currency, a $1 bill, for example, in each of the 23 $1 slots spread around the wheel.

A glass-covered table set in front of the wheel is where players place their bets. Pieces of currency, one to match each of the denominations around the wheel, are represented on this betting table layout. Players place their bets on top of their selection. A bet on the $1 bill will pay $1 for an even-money return if the spin of the wheel results in the leather strap stopping in the $1 bill slot.

A bet on the $2 bill pays off at 2 to 1. The $5 winner gets 5 to 1, the $10 winner receives odds of 10 to 1, and 20 to 1 odds go to the lucky player who selected the $20 denomination (if the wheel should stop in either of the two slots marked with a $20 bill).

If the player selects one of the special designs or joker designate, the payoff is 40 to 1. Each of these 40 to 1 selections is an individual bet. In all, there are seven choices for making a bet.

Figuring the Odds

To calculate the percentage in favor of the casino, we multiply each payoff symbol by its dollar value, subtract that from the remaining total number of symbols, and divide by 54. The $1 symbol gives us 23 chances of winning against 31 chances to lose. This leaves eight divided by 54.

The casino edge is 14.8%. The 15 $2 slots versus the 39 other chances give the house an edge of 16.7%. The eight $5 symbols, paying 5 to 1 odds, give the house an edge of 11.1%.

The four $10 slots paying off at 10 to 1 give the house an advantage of 18.5%. The two $20 slots with odds of 20 to 1, still provide a built-in edge of 22.2% in favor of the casino. Either choice of a single bet on the joker or special design slot work to a 24% house advantage.

Other combinations of denominations on the wheel will produce different house advantages...but now you know how to calculate the odds.

* * *

The attraction to the Wheel of Fortune is the aspect of fun and games. Patrons walking through the casino stop to watch the wheel as it spins and ticks, then stay to play a few dollars to see if their lucky guess produces a winner.

KEEPING YOUR GAMING KNOWLEDGE CURRENT THROUGH *WIN*

Now that you know how to play the games, you will want to keep abreast of all the latest rule variations in the games in casinos around the world. *WIN* Magazine (formerly *Gambling Times*)can give you that information.
WIN. Then you can always count on it being there, conveniently

Since February of 1977, readers of *WIN* Magazine (formerly *Gambling Times*) have profited immensely. They have done so by using the information they have read each month. if that sounds like a simple solution to winning more and losing less, well it is! Readers look to *WIN* for that very specific reason. And it delivers.

WIN is totally dedicated to showing readers how to win more money in every form of legalized gambling. How much you're going to win depends on many factors, but it's going to be considerably more than the cost of a subscription.

WIN will bring you the knowledge you need to come home a winner and come home in the money. For it is knowledge, the kind of knowledge you'll get in its pages, that separates winners from losers. It's winning and money that *WIN* offers you. *WIN* will be your working manual to winning wealth.

The current distribution of this magazine is limited to selected newsstands in selected cities. Additionally, at newstands where it is available, it's being snapped up, as soon as it's displayed, by gamblers who know a sure bet when they see one.

So if you're serious about winning, you're best off subscribing to *WIN*. Then you can always count on it being there, conveniently delivered to your mailbox—and what's more, it will be there one to two weeks before it appears on the newsstands. You'll be among the first to receive the current issue as soon as it comes off the presses, and being first is the way to be a winner.

163

Having every monthly issue of *WIN* will enable you to build an "Encyclopedia of Gambling," since the contents of this magazine are full of sound advice that will be as good in five or ten years as it is now.

As you can see, a subscription to *WIN* is your best bet for a future of knowledgeable gambling. It's your ticket to *WINNING* and *MONEY*.

Take the time to read the following offer. As you can see, *WIN* has gone all out to give you outstanding bonuses. You can join the knowledgeable players who have learned that *WIN* helps them to win more money.

NINE NEW WAYS TO GET 12 WINNING ISSUES OF *WIN* FREE...

Every month over 250,000 readers trust *WIN* to introduce powerful new winning strategies and systems. Using proven scientific methods, the world's leading experts show you how to win big money in the complex field of gambling.

WIN has shown how progressive slot machines can be beaten. Readers have discovered important new edges in blackjack. They've been shown how to know for sure when an opponent is bluffing at poker. *WIN* has also spelled out winning methods for football, baseball and basketball. They've published profound new ways of beating horses. Their team of experts will uncover information in the months ahead that's certain to be worth thousands of dollars to you.

In fact, the features are so revolutionary that they must take special precautions to make sure *WIN* readers learn these secrets long before anyone else. So how much is *WIN* worth to you? Well...

NOW *WIN* CAN BE BETTER THAN FREE! Here's how: This BONUS package comes AUTOMATICALLY TO YOU WHEN YOU SUBSCRIBE...or goes to a friend if you give a gift subscription.

★1. A CARD that entitles you to a 50% discount at over 2,000 quality hotels in over 400 cities, mainly in North America and the Caribbean. Only the finest hotels are included; chains such as Holiday Inn,

Sheraton, Hilton, Best Western, Marriott and Ramada Inns. Discounts are good 365 days per year. Stay as long as you like, subject to availability. Save as much as $100 per night.

★2. A 50% discount on a one week stay in over 2,000 condominiums, worldwide, including the United States, Canada, Mexico, France, Bahamas, Jamaica, Italy, Spain, Germany, Austria, Aruba and many more! Reservations made by a toll free number.

★3. Free Kodak film for life when you use our specified National Processing laboratory, which gives a 40% discount off Kodak list prices for developing. Free Kodak Color film, any size, speed or exposure to fit your camera, is provided with each roll of film developed.

★4. A 5% REBATE on the lowest available scheduled Airline fares in the US and up to a 45% REBATE on international flights when you book through our contract agency, San Diego Travel. Licensed and Bonded since 1963. Reservations can be made by a toll free number.

★5. A 3 day/2 night FREE vacation for two in your choice of Las Vegas, Reno, Tahoe, Atlantic City or Hawaii, plus Disneyland or DisneyWorld—when you book your air fare and reservations through our travel agency, San Diego Travel.

★6. A funpack booklet entitling the holder to over $250 in discounts at local businesses in your choice of: Las Vegas, Reno, Tahoe, Atlantic City, Hawaii, Orlando, Carlsbad-Oceanside, Disneyland, Palm Springs or Acapulco, Mexico. Includes cash, meals, chips, Keno, lucky bucks, slot tokens, drinks, entertainment, attractions and much, much more! Outside of Nevada the funpack may not include cash or gambling benefits. Good 7 days a week, including all holidays.

★7. 15% to 50% discounts on over 1,000 cruise trips. Savings can be as much as $1,000 per cruise. Includes a $50 per cabin bar-boutique ship credit. Reservations by toll free number.

★8. A standard discount on car rental from Hertz, Avis, Budget and Alamo car rental agencies. Guaranteed lowest prices, not available to the public. Toll free numbers in US & Canada.

★9. Your choice of a FREE 3-piece, 6-piece or all 9-piece set of English Leather Designer Luggage. Total value of all 9 pieces is $199.90. Gift certificate with each subscription.

To begin your delivery of *WIN* magazine at once, enclose a payment of $36.00 by check or money order (U.S. currency), Mastercard or Visa. Add $5.00 per year for postage outside the United States. Send payment to:

> *WIN* MAGAZINE
> 16760 Stagg St., Suite 213
> Van Nuys, CA 91406-1642

Other Valuable Sources of Knowledge Available Through *Gambling Times Inc.*

The following publications and books are available through Gambling Times Inc., 16760 Stagg St., Suite 213, Van Nuys, CA 91406.

The Experts Blackjack Newsletter.
This bi-monthly newsletter has all the top blackjack Experts working just for you. Features answers, strategies and insights that were never before possible. Yearly subscriptions are $30 for 6 issues.

OTHER *GAMBLING TIMES* BOOKS
AVAILABLE—CURRENT RELEASES

BLACKJACK BOOKS

The Beginner's Guide to Winning
Blackjack by Stanley Roberts
Gambling Times Guide to Blackjack
by Stanley Roberts
Winning Blackjack
by Stanley Roberts
Million Dollar Blackjack
by Ken Uston

POKER BOOKS

According to Doyle
by Doyle Brunson
Caro on Gambling
by Mike Caro
Caro's Book of Tells
by Mike Caro
Free Money: How to Win in the
Cardrooms of California
by Michael Wiesenberg
New Poker Games
by Mike Caro
Poker for Women
by Mike Caro
The Railbird
by Rex Jones
Tales Out of Tulsa
by Bobby Baldwin
Wins, Places and Pros
by Tex Sheahan

CASINO GAMING BOOKS

The GT Guide to Casino Games
by Len Miller
The GT Guide to Craps
by N.B. Winkless, Jr.
How to Win at Casino Gaming
Tournaments by Haven Earle Haley

GENERAL INTEREST BOOKS

Gambling and the Law
by I. Nelson Rose
The GT Guide to Bingo
by Roger Snowden
The GT Guide to European and Asian
Games by Syd Helprin
The GT Guide to Systems that Win, Vols.
I and II
The GT Guide to Winnings Systems, Vol. II
GT Presents Winning Systems and
Methods, Vols. I and II
The GT Quiz Book
by Mike Caro
Golf, Gambling and Gamesmanship
by Gary Moore
The Mathematics of Gambling
by Dr. Edward O. Thorp
P$yching Out Vegas
by Marvin Karlins, Ph.D.

Winning by Computer
by Dr. Donald Sullivan

SPORTS BETTING BOOKS

Fast Track to Thoroughbred Profits
by Mark Cramer
The GT Guide to Basketball Handicapping
by Barbara Nathan
The GT Guide to Football Handicapping
by Bob McCune
The GT Guide to Greyhound Racing
by William McBride
The GT Guide to Harness Racing
by Igor Kusyshyn, Ph.D., Al Stanley
and Sam Dragich
The GT Guide to Jai Alai
by William R. Keevers
The GT Guide to Thoroughbred Racing
by R.G. Denis

Gambling Books Ordering Information

Ask for any of the books listed below at your bookstore. Or to order direct from the publisher, call 1-800-447-BOOK (MasterCard or Visa), or send a check or money order for the books purchased (plus $4.00 shipping and handling for the first book ordered and $1.00 for each additional book) to Carol Publishing Group, 120 Enterprise Avenue, Dept. 70002, Secaucus, NJ 07094.

Beating the Wheel: The System That's Won More Than $6 Million, From Las Vegas to Monte Carlo by Russell T. Barnhart
$14.95 paper 0-8184-0553-8 (CAN $19.95)

Beat the House: Sixteen Ways to Win at Blackjack, Craps, Roulette, Baccarat and Other Table Games by Frederick Lembeck
$12.95 paper 0-8065-1607-0 (CAN $17.95)

Blackjack Your Way to Riches
by Richard Albert Canfield
$12.95 paper 0-8184-0498-1 (CAN $17.95)

The Cheapskate's Guide to Las Vegas: Hotels, Gambling, Food, Entertainment, and Much More by Connie Emerson
$10.95 paper 0-8065-1844-8 (CAN $14.95)

The Complete Book of Sports Betting: A New, No Nonsense Approach to Sports Betting by Jack Moore
$14.95 paper 0-8184-0579-1 (CAN $20.95)

Darwin Ortiz on Casino Gambling: The Complete Guide to Playing & Winning by Darwin Ortiz
$14.95 paper 0-8184-0525-2 (CAN $20.95)

For Winners Only: The Only Casino Gambling Guide You'll Ever Need by Peter J. Andrews
$18.95 paper 0-8065-1728-X (CAN $26.95)

Gambling Scams: How They Work, How to Detect Them, How to Protect Yourself by Darwin Ortiz
$12.95 paper 0-8184-0529-5 (CAN $15.95)

Gambling Times Guide to Blackjack
by Stanley Roberts
$12.95 paper 0-89746-015-4 (CAN $17.95)

How to Be Treated Like a High Roller
by Robert Renneisen
$8.95 paper 0-8184-0580-4 (CAN $12.95)

How to Win at Gin Rummy
by Pramod Shankar
$10.95 paper 0-8184-0586-4 (CAN $14.95)

John Patrick's Advanced Blackjack
$19.95 paper 0-8184-0582-1 (CAN $27.95)

John Patrick's Advanced Craps
$18.95 paper 0-8184-0577-5 (CAN $26.95)

John Patrick's Blackjack
$14.95 paper 0-8184-0555-4 (CAN $19.95)

John Patrick's Craps
$16.95 paper 0-8184-0554-6 (CAN $20.95)

John Patrick's Roulette
$16.95 paper 0-8184-0587-2 (CAN $22.95)

John Patrick's Slots
$12.95 paper 0-8184-0574-0 (CAN $17.95)

Million Dollar Blackjack by Ken Uston
$18.95 paper 0-89746-068-5 (CAN $26.95)

Playing Blackjack as a Business
by Lawrence Revere
$15.95 paper 0-8184-0064-1 (CAN $21.95)

Progression Blackjack: Exposing the Cardcounting Myth by Donald Dahl
$11.95 paper 0-8065-1396-9 (CAN $16.95)

Slot Smarts by Claude Halcombe
$9.95 paper 0-8184-0584-8 (CAN $13.95)

The Ultimate Blackjack Book
by Walter Thomason
$14.95 paper 0-8184-0589-9 (CAN $19.95)

Win at Video Poker: The Guide to Beating the Poker Machines by Roger Fleming
$10.95 paper 0-8065-1605-4 (CAN $14.95)

Winning at Slot Machines by Jim Regan
$7.95 paper 0-8065-0973-2 (CAN $10.95)

Winning Blackjack in Atlantic City and Around the World by Thomas Gaffney
$7.95 paper 0-8065-1178-8 (CAN $10.95)

Winning Blackjack Without Counting Cards
by David S. Popik
$9.95 paper 0-8065-0963-5 (CAN $13.95)

(Prices subject to change; books subject to availability)